U.S. MILITARY POCKET

SURVIVAL GUIDE

U.S. MILITARY POCKET
SURVIVAL
GUIDE

ARMY, MARINE CORPS, NAVY, AND AIR FORCE

REVISED AND UPDATED BY
SERGEANT FIRST CLASS MATT LARSEN

The Lyons Press
Guilford, Connecticut
An imprint of The Globe Pequot Press

Copyright © 2009 by Morris Book Publishing, LLC

The Lyons Press is an imprint of The Globe Pequot Press.

Text designed by Libby Kingsbury

Library of Congress Cataloging-in-Publication Data is available on file.

ISBN 978-1-59921-487-0

Printed in the United States of America

10 9 8 7 6

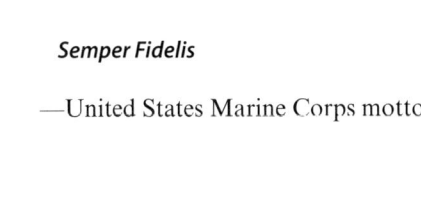

Semper Fidelis

—United States Marine Corps motto

CONTENTS

CHAPTER X INDUCED CONDITIONS

LIST OF ILLUSTRATIONS

QUICK REFERENCE CHECKLIST

Preparation is what we have left when the plan falls apart. Acquiring the skills necessary for survival is a part of this preparation. However, it takes much more than the knowledge and skills to build shelters, find food, make fires and travel without the aid of standard navigational devices to live successfully through a survival or evasion situation. Some people with little or no survival training have managed to survive life-threatening circumstances. Some people with survival training have not used their skills and have died. A key ingredient in any survival situation is the mental attitude of the people involved. Having survival skills and proper preparation are important. Having the will to survive is essential. Without a desire to survive, acquired skills serve little purpose and invaluable knowledge goes to waste.

Decide to Survive!

The first step in any survival situation is to decide to survive. The very nature of any survival situation is to seem hopeless. It is easy to become overwhelmed by it. You must make a conscious effort to decide that you will survive; it is never hopeless until you give up the fight. Once the decision to survive has been made, let the word SURVIVAL be your guide. It is the basis for everything presented in this book. It is a good idea to memorize what each of the letters stands for so that you will have them with you no matter what.

S	Size up the situation, surroundings, physical condition, equipment.
U	Use all your senses. Undue haste makes waste.
R	Remember where you are.
V	Vanquish fear and panic.
I	Improvise and improve.
V	Value living.
A	Act like the natives.
L	Live by your wits.

1. Immediate Actions

Survival situations never happen because of a plan that went right. Contingency planning is important but it is impossible to predict everything that may go wrong. You can, however, prepare yourself for the unpredictability of life in many ways. Do you know the route? Are you familiar with the terrain? Are you fit? Did you bring equipment to handle contingencies? Remember that preparation is what you have left when plans go bad.

The actions that you take immediately when you find yourself in a potential survival situation are the most important decisions of your life and can make the difference between life and death. If you have prepared yourself wisely, you will make better decisions in a pinch.

a. Assess immediate situation. THINK BEFORE YOU ACT!
b. Seek a concealed site.
c. Assess medical condition; treat as necessary (Chapter V).
d. Sanitize uniform of potentially compromising information.
e. Sanitize area; hide equipment you are leaving.
f. Apply personal camouflage.
g. Move away from concealed site; use counter-tracking techniques.
h. Use terrain to advantage, for communication and concealment.
i. Find a hole-up site.
j. Take action to protect yourself from nuclear, biological, or chemical hazards (Chapter IX).

2. Hole-Up Site (Chapter I)

A hole-up site is just what it says, a place to "hole up" while you make initial plans and prepare yourself to carry them out.

a. Reassess situation; treat injuries, then inventory equipment.

b. Review plan of action; establish priorities
   (Chapter VI).
c. Determine current location.
d. Improve camouflage.
e. Focus thoughts on task(s) at hand.
f. Execute plan of action. Stay flexible!

3. Concealment (Chapter I)
Concealment is protection from enemy observation.

a. Select a place of concealment providing:
   (1) Adequate concealment, ground and air.
   (2) Safe distance from enemy positions and lines of
       communications (LOC).
   (3) Listening and observation points.
   (4) Multiple avenues of escape.
   (5) Protection from the environment.
   (6) Possible communications/signaling opportunities.

b. Stay alert, maintain security.
c. Drink water.

4. Movement (Chapters I and II)
In a non-tactical setting it is seldom wise to move during
a survival situation other than to avoid an immediately
threatening situation.

a. Travel slowly and deliberately.
b. DO NOT leave evidence of travel; use noise and light
   discipline.
c. Stay away from LOC.
d. Stop, look, listen, and smell; take appropriate action(s).
e. Move from one concealed area to another.
f. Use evasion movement techniques (Chapter I).

5.Communications and Signaling (Chapter III)
Communication is the key to recovery.

a. *Communicate as directed in applicable plans/orders, particularly when considering transmitting in the blind.*
b. *Be prepared to use communications and signaling devices on short notice.*
c. *Use of communications and signaling devices may compromise position.*

6. Recovery (Chapter IV)
Recovery can be one of the most dangerous times when surviving in a hostile environment.

a. *Select site(s) IAW criteria in theater recovery plans.*
b. *Ensure site is free of hazards; secure personal gear.*
c. *Select best area for communications and signaling devices.*
d. *Observe site for proximity to enemy activity and LOC.*
e. *Follow recovery force instructions.*

U.S. MILITARY POCKET

SURVIVAL GUIDE

CHAPTER I

EVASION

1. PLANNING   It is a common mistake when planning an operation to give short shrift to the evasion plan. This mistake, which often leads to disaster, happens because commanders are naturally focused on mission accomplishment. Planning contingencies in case of failure is easy to push off to the very last priority. Your evasion plan is also the coordinating document for rescue efforts. If it is not well thought out, the temptation to deviate from it, and therefore throw off all of your coordination with rescue efforts, will be great.

a. Review the quick reference checklist on the inside cover.
b. Guidelines for successful evasion include:
   1. Keeping a positive attitude.
   2. Using established procedures.
   3. Following your evasion plan of action.
   4. Being patient.
   5. Drinking water (*DO NOT* eat food without water).
   6. Conserving strength for critical periods.
   7. Resting and sleeping as much as possible.
   8. Staying out of sight.
   9. Not leaving an obvious trail.

c. The following odors stand out and may give an evader away:
   1. Scented soaps and shampoos.
   2. Shaving cream, aftershave lotion, or other cosmetics.

3. Insect repellent (camouflage stick is least scented).
4. Gum and candy (smell is strong or sweet).
5. Tobacco (odor is unmistakable).
6. Body odor (clean yourself when possible).

d. Where to go (initiate evasion plan of action):
1. Near a suitable area for recovery.
2. Selected area for evasion.
3. Neutral or friendly country or area.
4. Designated area for recovery.

2. CAMOUFLAGE Hiding from the enemy, blending in with your environment, and concealing what you do all take planning and constant vigilance. You must know and have practiced the art of camouflage before you need it to be effective.

a. Basic principles:
1. Hide. Utilize natural setting when possible.
2. Blend. Color and texture must match surroundings.
3. Disturb as little as possible.
4. Avoid activity that reveals movement to the enemy.
5. Pay close attention to detail. Apply personal camouflage.

b. Camouflage patterns (Figure I-1):
1. Blotch pattern.
   - Temperate deciduous (leaf shedding) areas.
   - Desert areas (barren).
   - Snow (barren).

2. Slash pattern.
   - Coniferous areas (broad slashes).
   - Jungle areas (broad slashes).
   - Grass (narrow slashes).

3. Combination. May use blotched and slash together.

| BLOTCH | SLASH |

Figure I-1. Camouflage Patterns

c. Personal camouflage application follows:

1. *Face.* Use dark colors on high spots and light colors on any remaining exposed areas. Use a hat, netting, or mask if available.
2. *Ears.* The insides and the backs should have two colors to break up outlines.
3. *Head, neck, hands, and the under chin.* Use scarf, collar, vegetation, netting, or coloration methods.
4. *Light colored hair.* Give special attention to conceal with a scarf or mosquito head net.

d. Position and movement camouflage follows:

1. Avoid unnecessary movement.
2. Take advantage of natural concealment:
   - Cut foliage fades and wilts, change regularly.
   - Change camouflage depending on the surroundings.
   - *DO NOT* select vegetation from same source.
   - Use stains from grasses, berries, dirt, and charcoal.

3. *DO NOT* over camouflage.
4. Match the light shades; the most common mistake is to be too dark.
5. Remember when using shadows, they shift with the sun.
6. Never expose shiny objects (like a watch, glasses, or pens).
7. Ensure watch alarms and hourly chimes are turned off.
8. Remove unit patches, name tags, rank insignia, etc.
9. Break up the outline of the body, "V" of crotch/ armpits.
10. Conduct observation from a prone and concealed position.

3. SHELTERS   Shelter from the elements can be an immediate necessity in many environments. In others it can simply be a method to maintain a good covered and concealed position while awaiting rescue. With either scenario it must be well thought out in order to provide what the evader requires with the appropriate amount of effort and without aiding the enemy in their search efforts.

a. Use camouflage and concealment.
b. Locate carefully. Easy-to-remember acronym: BLISS.

B	Blend
L	Low silhouette
I	Irregular shape
S	Small
S	Secluded location

c. DO NOT create a trail by coming and going on the same route:
1. Choose an area:

- Least likely to be searched (drainages, rough terrain, etc.) and blends with the environment.
- With escape routes (*DO NOT* corner yourself).
- With observable approaches.

2. Locate entrances and exits in brush and along ridges, ditches, and rocks to keep from forming paths to site.
3. Be wary of flash floods in ravines and canyons.
4. Conceal with minimal to no preparation.
5. Take the direction-finding threat into account before transmitting from shelter.
6. Ensure overhead concealment.
7. Plan to conceal your shelter when you leave.

4. MOVEMENT   There is a natural tendency, especially with the driven and adventuresome who find themselves in an evasion situation, to want to move. Movement, however, if poorly planned or executed can simply make the enemy's job of finding you much easier. Not only where to go but every aspect of how to get there must be considered.

a. A moving object is easy to spot. If travel is necessary:
1. Mask with natural cover (**Figure I-2**).
2. Use the military crest.
3. Restrict to periods of low light, bad weather, wind, or reduced enemy activity.
4. Remember counter tracking.
5. Avoid silhouetting (**Figure I-3**).
6. At irregular intervals:
   - *STOP* at a point of concealment, occasionally watching over your back trail.
   - *LOOK* for signs of human or animal activity (smoke, tracks, roads, troops, vehicles, aircraft, wire, buildings, etc.).

Figure I-2. Ground Movement

- Watch for trip wires or booby traps and avoid leaving evidence of travel. Peripheral vision is more effective for recognizing movement at night and twilight. Watch for signs of someone following your trail.
- *LISTEN* for vehicles, troops, aircraft, weapons, animals, etc.
- *SMELL* for vehicles, troops, animals, fires, etc.
- Employ noise discipline; check clothing and equipment for items that could make noise during movement and secure them.

b. Break up the human shape or recognizable lines.

c. Route selection requires detailed planning and special techniques (irregular route/zigzag) to camouflage evidence of travel.

d. Some techniques for concealing evidence of travel follow:

1. Avoid disturbing the vegetation above knee level.
2. *DO NOT* break branches, leaves, or grass.
3. Use a walking stick to part vegetation and push it back to its original position.
4. *DO NOT* grab small trees or brush. (This may scuff the bark or create movement that is easily spotted. In snow country, this creates a path of snowless vegetation revealing your route.)
5. Pick firm footing (carefully place the foot lightly but squarely on the surface to avoid slipping). *TRY NOT TO*:
   - Overturn ground cover, rocks, and sticks.
   - Scuff bark on logs and sticks.
   - Make noise by breaking sticks. (Cloth wrapped around feet helps muffle this.)

Figure I-3. Avoid Silhouetting

- Mangle grass and bushes that normally spring back.
6. Mask unavoidable tracks in soft footing by:
   - Placing tracks in the shadows of vegetation, downed logs, and snowdrifts.
   - Moving before and during precipitation allows tracks to fill in.
   - Traveling during windy periods.
   - Taking advantage of solid surfaces (logs, rocks, etc.), leaving less evidence of travel.
   - Patting out tracks lightly to speed their break-down or make them look old.
7. Secure trash or loose equipment; hide or bury discarded items. (Trash or lost equipment identifies who lost it.)
8. Concentrate on defeating the handler if pursued by dogs.

e. Penetrate obstacles as follows:
1. Enter deep ditches feet first to avoid injury.
2. Go around chain-link and wire fences. Go under fence if unavoidable, crossing at damaged areas.

Figure I-4. Rail Fences

DO NOT touch fence; look for electrical insulators or security devices.

3. Penetrate rail fences, passing under or between lower rails. If impractical, go over the top, presenting as low a silhouette as possible **(Figure I-4).**

4. Cross roads after observation from concealment to determine enemy activity. Cross at points offering concealment such as bushes, shadows, bend in road, etc. When possible, cross in a manner leaving

Figure I-5. Road Crossing

Figure I-6. Railroad Tracks

your footprints parallel (walking along the road for a short distance or cross step sideways) to the road. (Figure I-5).

5. Use same method of observation for railroad tracks that was used for roads. Next, align body parallel to tracks with face down, cross tracks using a semi-push-up motion. Repeat for the second track. (Figure I-6).

WARNING: If three rails exist, one may be electrified.

CHAPTER II

NAVIGATION

Assess the threat and apply appropriate evasion principles.

1. STAY OR MOVE CONSIDERATIONS   Your best chance of recovery comes as soon as recovery elements can arrive at your vehicle/aircraft site. In a noncombat environment only extraordinary circumstances should compel you to leave this site. During combat, however, it is very likely that any enemy in the area will be racing the rescuers to get you. Knowing when the situation demands that you move or stay put will be critical.

a. Stay with the vehicle/aircraft in a noncombat environment.
b. Leave only when:
 1. Dictated by the threat, including the increased likelihood of compromise.
 2. Are certain of your location, have a known destination, and have the ability to get there.
 3. Can reach water, food, shelter, and/or help.
 4. Convinced rescue is not coming.

c. Consider the following if you decide to travel:
 1. Follow the briefed evasion plan.
 2. Determine which direction to travel and why.
 3. Decide what equipment to take, cache, or destroy.

d. Leave information at your starting point (in a noncombat environment) that includes:
1. Destination.
2. Route of travel.
3. Personal condition.
4. Supplies available.

e. Consider the following for maps or GPS (in a combat environment):
1. *DO NOT* write on the map.
2. *DO NOT* soil the map by touching the destination.
3. *DO NOT* fold in a manner providing travel information.
4. *DO NOT* use waypoint or other features on GPS to mark locations.
5. Conserve GPS batteries.

Note: These actions may compromise information if captured.

2. NAVIGATION AND POSITION DETERMINATION Once the decision has been made to move, you must know where you are and where you want to go. As simple as this sounds, if you have not kept track before you are in trouble. Figuring out where you are is one of the more difficult things in a real situation.

a. Determine your general location by:
1. Developing a working knowledge of the operational area.
   - Geographic checkpoints.
   - Man-made checkpoints.
   - Previous knowledge of operational area.

2. Using the Rate x Time = Distance formula.
3. Using information provided in the map legend.

4. Using prominent landmarks.
5. Visualizing map to determine position.

b. Determine cardinal directions (north, south, east, and west) by:

1. Using compass.
   CAUTION: The following methods are *NOT* highly accurate and give only general cardinal direction.
2. Using stick and shadow method to determine a true north-south line (**Figure II-1**).
3. Remembering the sunrise/moonrise is in the east and sunset/moonset is in the west.

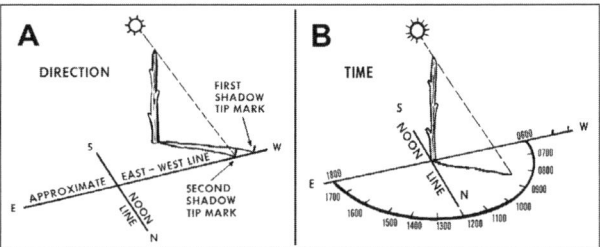

Figure II-1. Stick and Shadow Method

4. Using a wristwatch to determine general cardinal direction (**Figure II-2**).
   - Digital watches. Visualize a clock face on the watch.
   - Northern Hemisphere. Point hour hand at the sun. South is halfway between the hour hand and 12 o'clock position.
   - Southern Hemisphere. Point the 12 o'clock position on your watch at the sun. North is halfway between the 12 o'clock position and the hour hand.

Figure II-2. Direction Using a Watch

5. Using a pocket navigator (**Figure II-3**):
   • Gather the following necessary materials:
     Flat writing material (such as an MRE box).
     1-2 inch shadow tip device (a twig, nail, or match).
     Pen or pencil.

   • Start construction at sunup; end construction at sundown. Do the following:
     Attach shadow tip device in center of paper.
     Secure navigator on flat surface (DO NOT move during setup period).
     Mark tip of shadow every 30 minutes, annotating the time.
     Connect marks to form an arc.
     Indicate north with a drawn arrow.

Note: The shortest line between base of shadow tip device and curved line is a north-south line.

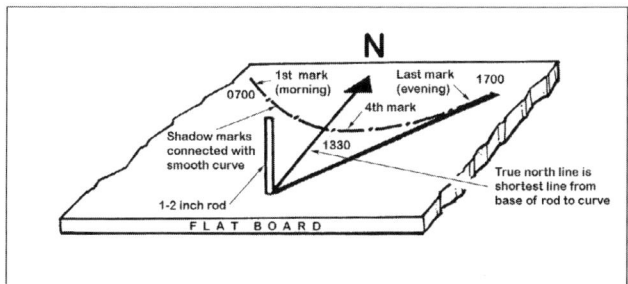

Figure II-3. Pocket Navigator

- Do the following during travel:

  Hold navigator so the shadow aligns with mark of present time (drawn arrow now points to true north).

- Remember the navigator is current for approximately one week.

  CAUTION: The Pocket Navigator is *NOT* recommended if evading.

6. Using the stars **(Figure II-4)**, the:
   - North Star is used to locate true north-south line.
   - Southern Cross is used to locate true south-north line.

c. Orient the map by:
1. Using a true north-south line **(Figure II-5)**:
   - Unfold map and place on a firm, flat, level non-metallic surface.
   - Align the compass on a true north-south line.

Figure II-4. Stars

Figure II-5. Orienting a Map Using a True North-South Line

- Rotate map and compass until stationary index line aligns with the magnetic variation indicated in marginal information.

  Easterly (subtract variation from 360 degrees).
  Westerly (add variation to 360 degrees).

2. Using a compass rose (**Figure II-6**):
   - Place edge of the lensatic compass on magnetic north line of the compass rose closest to your location.

Star indicates magnetic line on EVC Chart.

Figure II-6. Map Orientation with Compass Rose

- Rotate map and compass until compass reads 360 degrees.

3. If there is NO compass, orient map using cardinal direction obtained by the stick and shadow method or the celestial aids (stars) method.

d. Determine specific location.
1. Global Positioning System (GPS).
   - DO NOT use GPS for primary navigation.

- Use GPS to confirm your position ONLY.
- Select area providing maximum satellite reception.
- Conserve GPS battery life.

2. Triangulation (resection) with a compass (FIGURE II-7).
   - Try to use three or more azimuths.
   - Positively identify a major land feature and determine a line of position (LOP).
   - Check map orientation each time compass is used.
   - Plot the LOP using a thin stick or blade of grass (combat) or pencil line (noncombat).
   - Repeat steps (b) through (d) for other LOPs.

e. Use the compass for night navigation by:
   Setting up compass for night navigation (FIGURE II-8).
   Aligning north-seeking arrow with luminous line and following front of compass.
   Using point-to-point navigation.

Figure II-7. Triangulation

Setting the Compass for Night Travel

Follow Front of Compass

6000

4000

2000

METERS 1:50000

0

Luminous Line

North-Seeking Arrow

Stationary Index

Bezel Ring

Each click of the bezel ring equals 3 degrees.

Heading between 0 and 180 degrees is divided by 3. Sum is number of clicks to the left of stationary index line. Heading between 180 and 360 degrees, subtract heading from 360 then divide sum by 3. New sum is the number of clicks to the right from stationary index line.

EXAMPLES

Heading of 027 degrees = 9 clicks left.
Heading of 300 degrees = 20 clicks right.

Figure II-8. Compass Night Navigation Setup

f. Route selection techniques follow:

1. Circumnavigation.
   - Find a prominent landmark on the opposite side of the obstacle.
   - Contour around obstacle to landmark.
   - Resume your route of travel.

2. Dogleg and 90 degree offset (**Figure II-9**).
3. Straight-line heading as follows:
   - Maintain heading until reaching destination.
   - Measure distance by counting the number of paces in a given course and convert to map units.

     One pace is the distance covered each time the same foot touches the ground.

     Distances measured by paces are approximate (example in open terrain, 900 paces per kilometer [average], or in rough terrain, 1200 paces per kilometer [average]).

   - Use pace count in conjunction with terrain evaluation and heading to determine location. An individual's pace varies because of factors such as steep terrain, day/night travel, or injured/

Figure II-9. Dogleg and 90 Degree Offset

uninjured condition. Adjust estimation of distance traveled against these factors to get relative accuracy when using a pace count.

4. Deliberate offset is:
   - Used when finding a point on a linear feature (that is, road or river).
   - Intentionally navigated to left or right of target so you know which way to turn at the linear feature.

5. Point-to-point is same as straight line.
   - Pick out landmarks on the heading and walk the trail of least resistance to a point.
   - On reaching a point, establish another landmark and continue.

3. TRAVEL CONSIDERATIONS There are many dangers that will need to be planned for while moving, from exposing yourself to the enemy to the possibility of injury while covering rough terrain. Making a realistic assessment of the risks and planning accordingly is the key to success.

a. Pick the easiest and safest route (noncombat).
b. Maintain a realistic pace; take rest stops when needed.
c. Avoid overdressing and overheating. Even in cold weather overheating can be a major problem.
d. Consider food and water requirements.
e. Take special care of feet (change socks regularly).
f. Pack equipment to prevent loss, damage, pack imbalance, and personal safety.
g. Go around obstacles, not over or through them.
h. Travel on trails whenever possible (noncombat).
i. Travel in forested areas if possible.
j. Avoid creek bottoms and ravines with NO escape in the event of heavy rains.

k. Consider the following for swamps, lakes, and unfordable rivers:
1. Circumnavigate swamps, lakes, and bogs if needed.
2. Travel downstream to find people and slower water.
3. Travel upstream to find narrower and shallow water.

4. RIVER TRAVEL   River travel may be faster and save energy when hypothermia is not a factor. It may be a primary mode of travel and LOC in a tropical environment (use with caution if evading).

a. Use flotation device (raft, log, bamboo, etc.).
b. Use a pole to move the raft in shallow water.
c. Use an oar in deep water.
d. Stay near inside edge of river bends (current speed is less).
e. Keep near shore.
f. Watch for the following DANGERS:
1. Snags.
2. Sweepers (overhanging limbs and trees).
3. Rapids (DO NOT attempt to shoot the rapids).
4. Waterfalls.
5. Hazardous animals.

g. Consider using a flotation device when crossing rivers or large/deep streams.

5. ICE AND SNOW TRAVEL   Traveling in winter conditions can either be very easy or very dangerous. It is important to know the hazards and to plan to avoid them.

Travel should be limited to areas free of hazards.

a. DO NOT travel in:
1. Blizzards.

2. Bitterly cold winds.
3. Poor visibility.

b. Obstacles to winter travel:
1. Reduced daylight hours (*BE AWARE*).
2. Deep soft snow (if movement is necessary, make snowshoes [**Figure II-10**]). Travel is easier in early morning or late afternoon near dusk when snow is frozen or crusted.
3. Avalanche prone areas to avoid:
   - Slopes 30 to 45 degrees or greater.
   - Trees without uphill branches (identifies prior avalanches).
   - Heavy snow loading on ridgetops.
4. If caught in an avalanche, do the following:
   - Backstroke to decrease burial depth.
   - Move hand around face to create air pocket as moving snow slows.

The snowshoe binding must be secured to the snowshoe so that the survivor's foot can pivot when walking.

Binding — make as shown from continuous length of split harness webbing or from suspension lines (braided lines preferred).

Figure II-10. Improvised Snowshoes

5. Frozen water crossings.
   - Weak ice should be expected where—
        Rivers are straight.
        Objects protrude through ice.
        Snowbanks extend over the ice.
        Rivers or streams come together.
        Water vapor rising indicates open or warm areas.
   - Air pockets form when a frozen river loses volume.
   - When crossing frozen water, distribute your weight by lying flat, belly crawling, or using snowshoes.

c. Glacier travel is hazardous and should be avoided.

6. MOUNTAIN HAZARDS Travel in mountainous areas presents its own difficulties and dangers.

a. Lightning. Avoid ridgetops during thunderstorms.
b. Avalanche. Avoid areas prone to avalanches.
c. Flash floods. Avoid low areas.
d. Easily predictable routes.

7. SUMMER HAZARDS (See page 22; Travel Considerations, items h through k.)
   1. Dense brush.
      - Travel on trails when possible (noncombat).
      - Travel in forested areas if possible.
      - Avoid creek bottoms and ravines with no escape in the event of heavy rains.

   2. Swamps, lakes, and unfordable rivers.
      - Circumnavigate swamps, lakes, and bogs if needed.
      - Travel downstream to find people and slower water.

- Travel upstream to find narrower and shallow water.

8. DRY CLIMATES   It is not only the heat that can affect you when traveling in dry climates. It is important to take prudent precautions even when the weather feels temperate or cold. Dehydration is a significant danger in a cold and dry environment because you will not feel the desire to drink as much water as the dry air is taking out of you.

a. DO NOT travel unless certain of reaching the destination using the water supply available.
b. Travel at dawn or dusk on hot days.
c. Follow the easiest trail possible (noncombat), avoiding—
    1. Deep sandy dune areas.
    2. Rough terrain.

d. In sand dune areas—
    1. Follow hard valley floor between dunes.
    2. Travel on the windward side of dune ridges.

e. If a sandstorm occurs:
    1. Mark your direction of travel.
    2. Sit or lie down in direction of travel.
    3. Try to get to the downwind side of natural shelter.
    4. Cover the mouth and nose with a piece of cloth.
    5. Protect the eyes.
    6. Remain stationary until the storm is over.

9. TROPICAL CLIMATES   In tropical climates it is not only uneven terrain and becoming a cold/heat casualty that you must be careful to avoid. Wise route selection and movement techniques can help you avoid the dangers presented by the more hostile forms of plant and animal life. If you plan your route poorly, terrain and vegetation can be an insurmountable obstacle to travel.

Figure II-11. Sea Anchor Deployment

a. *Travel only when it is light.*

b. *Avoid obstacles like thickets and swamps.*

c. *Part the vegetation to pass through. Avoid grabbing vegetation; it may have spines or thorns (use gloves if possible).*

d. *DO NOT climb over logs if you can go around them.*

e. *Find trails—*

    1. Where two streams meet.

    2. Where a low pass goes over a range of hills.

f. *While traveling trails:*

    1. Watch for disturbed areas on game trails; they may indicate a pitfall or trap.

    2. Use a walking stick to probe for pitfalls or traps.

    3. DO NOT sleep on the trail.

    4. Exercise caution; the enemy uses the trails also.

10. OPEN SEAS You should only attempt to travel in a survival situation over the open sea under the direst circumstances because of the vagaries of current and wind. Navigation is difficult at the best of times and only becomes more difficult with field expedient methods.

a. Using currents:

1. Deploy sea anchor (Figure II-11). Sea anchor may be adjusted to make use of existing currents.
2. Sit low in the raft.
3. Deflate the raft slightly so it rides lower in the water.

b. Using winds:

1. Pull in sea anchor.
2. Inflate raft so it rides higher.
3. Sit up in raft so body catches the wind.
4. Construct a shade cover/sail (Figure II-12). (Sail aids in making landfall.)

c. Making landfall. Indications of land are:

1. Fixed cumulus clouds in a clear sky or in a cloudy sky where all other clouds are moving.
2. Greenish tint in the sky (in the tropics).
3. Lighter colored reflection on clouds; open water causes dark gray reflections (in the arctic).

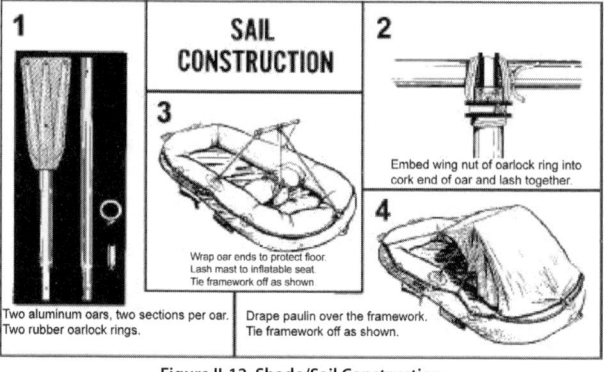

Figure II-12. Shade/Sail Construction

4. Lighter colored water (indicates shallow water).
5. The odors and sounds.
   * Odors from swamps and smoke.
   * Roar of surf, bird cries coming from one direction.
6. Directional flights of birds at dawn and at dusk.

d. Swimming ashore:
1. Consider physical condition.
2. Use a flotation aid.
3. Secure all gear to body before reaching landfall.
4. Remain in raft as long as possible.
5. Use the sidestroke or breaststroke to conserve strength if thrown from raft.
6. Wear footgear and at least one layer of clothing.
7. Try to make landfall during the lull between the sets of waves (waves are generally in sets of seven, from smallest to largest).
8. In moderate surf.
   * Swim forward on the back of a wave.
   * Make a shallow dive just before the wave breaks to end the ride.

9. In high surf.
   * Swim shoreward in the trough between waves.
   * When the seaward wave approaches, face it and submerge.
   * After it passes, work shoreward in the next trough.
10. If caught in the undertow of a large wave—
    * Remain calm and swim to the surface.
    * Lie as close to the surface as possible.
    * Parallel shoreline and attempt landfall at a point further down shore.

11. Select a landing point.
    * Avoid places where waves explode upon rocks.

- Find a place where waves smoothly rush onto the rocks.

12. After selecting a landing site:
    - Face shoreward.
    - Assume a sitting position with feet 2 or 3 feet lower than head to absorb the shock of hitting submerged objects.

e. Rafting ashore:
1. Select landing point carefully.
2. Use caution landing when the sun is low and straight in front of you causing poor visibility.
3. Land on the lee (downwind) side of islands or point of land if possible.
4. Head for gaps in the surf line.
5. Penetrate surf by—
   - Taking down most shade/sails.
   - Using paddles to maintain control.
   - Deploying a sea anchor for stability.

   CAUTION: DO NOT deploy a sea anchor if traveling through coral.

f. Making sea ice landings on large stable ice flows. Icebergs, small flows, and disintegrating flows are dangerous (ice can cut a raft).
1. Use paddles to avoid sharp edges.
2. Store raft away from the ice edge.
3. Keep raft inflated and ready for use.
4. Weight down/secure raft so it does not blow away.

11. COUNTER TRACKING It is important to remember that no matter what terrain you are moving through, in an evasion situation, the enemy can only track you if they pick up your trail. The very best counter-tracking technique is to think about what you are leaving as you pass. If it is something noticeable and out of the ordinary, you can assume that is where the enemy will begin tracking you.

a. Assume you are being tracked.
1. Plan your stops with counter tracking in mind. Tracking will usually begin where you have left some obvious sign, such as an un-camouflaged camp or fire site.
2. Pay attention to what you leave behind. Obvious signs will invite trackers.

b. Speed makes tracking you easier. When you are moving fast, you pay little attention to the obvious trail you are leaving behind you.

c. Reduce, conceal, and disguise the signs you leave.
1. Use hard ground for movement when available.
2. Blend with signs left by local population.
3. Plan your stops by thinking about what sign it will leave.

CHAPTER III

RADIO COMMUNICATIONS AND SIGNALING

Inventory and review the operating instructions of all communications and signaling equipment.

1. RADIO COMMUNICATIONS (VOICE AND DATA)

a. Noncombat.
1. Ensure locator beacon is operational.
2. Follow standing plans for on/off operations to conserve battery use.

b. Combat.
1. Turn off locator beacon.
2. Keep it with you to supplement radio communications.
3. Follow plans/orders for on/off operations.

c. Make initial contact as soon as possible or as directed in applicable plans/orders.
d. If no immediate contact, then as directed in applicable plans/orders.
e. Locate spare radio and batteries (keep warm and dry).
f. Transmissions.
1. Use concealment sites (combat) that optimize line of site (LOS).
2. Face recovery asset.
3. Keep antenna perpendicular to intended receiver (FIGURE III-1).

4. DO NOT ground antenna (that is finger on antenna or attaching bolt, space blanket, vegetation, etc.).
5. Keep transmissions short (3-5 seconds maximum). Use data burst if available.
6. Move after each transmission (ONLY in combat, if possible).
7. If transmitting in the blind, ensure a clear LOS towards the equator.
8. Use terrain masking to hinder enemy direction finding.

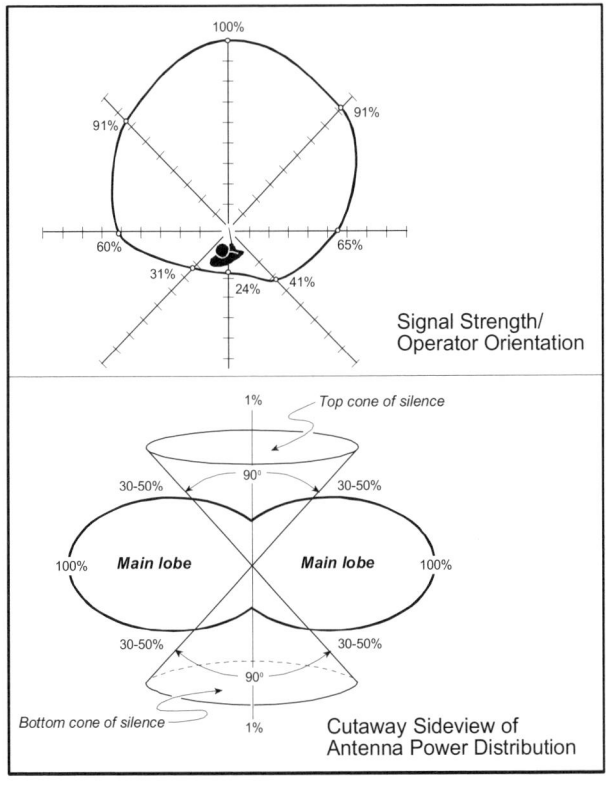

Figure III-1. Radio Transmission Characteristics

g. Listening (use reception times in applicable plans/orders or as directed by recovery forces).

2. SIGNALING

a. Pyrotechnic signals.
1. Prepare early (weather permitting).
2. Use as directed in applicable plans/orders or as directed by recovery forces.
3. Extend over raft's edge before activating.

b. Signal mirror (Figure III-2).
1. Use as directed by recovery forces.
2. If no radio, use only with confirmed friendly forces.
3. Cover when not in use.

Note: Make a mirror from any shiny metal or glass.

c. Strobe/IR lights.
1. Prepare early, consider filters and shields.
2. Use as directed by recovery forces.
3. Conserve battery life.

Note: Produces one residual flash when turned off.

Figure III-2. Sighting Techniques

Figure III-3. Size and Ratio

d. Pattern signals (use as directed in applicable plans/orders).
1. Materials:
   - Man-made (space blanket, signal paulin, parachute).
   - Natural materials that contrast the color and/or texture of the signaling area (rocks, brush, branches, stomped grass).
2. Location.
   - Maximize visibility from above.
   - Provide concealment from ground observation.
3. Size (large as possible) and ratio (**Figure III-3**).
4. Shape (maintain straight lines and sharp corners).
5. Contrast (use color and shadows).
6. Pattern signals (**Figure III-4**).

e. Sea dye marker.
1. DO NOT waste in rough seas or fast moving water.
2. Conserve unused dye by rewrapping.
3. May be used to color snow.

f. Noncombat considerations:
1. Use a fire at night.
2. Use smoke for day (tires or petroleum products for dark smoke and green vegetation for light smoke) (**Figure III-5**).
3. Use signal mirror to sweep horizon.
4. Use audio signals (that is, voice, whistle, and weapons fire).

NO.	MESSAGE	CODE SYMBOL
1	REQUIRE ASSISTANCE	V
2	REQUIRE MEDICAL ASSISTANCE	X
3	NO or NEGATIVE	N
4	YES or AFFIRMATIVE	Y
5	PROCEEDING IN THIS DIRECTION	↑

Figure III-4. Signal Key

LOTS OF DEAD DRY TWIGS OR KINDLING FOR QUICK STARTING FAST-BURNING FIRE

EVERGREEN BOUGHS

SMALL OPENING FOR LIGHTING FIRE

Figure III-5. Smoke Generator

CHAPTER IV

RECOVERY

1. RESPONSIBILITIES You must have a clear understanding of what is expected of you and what you can expect from others. Any linkup operation is dangerous because of the uncertainty of the situation and apprehension of everyone involved. The best tools to mitigate the risks are good communication and for everyone involved to be familiar with established procedures.

a. Establish radio contact with recovery forces (if possible).

b. Maintain communication with recovery forces until recovered.

c. Be prepared to authenticate as directed in applicable plans/ orders.

d. Follow recovery force instructions; be prepared to report—

    1. Enemy activity in the recovery area.

    2. Recovery site characteristics (slope, obstacles, size, etc.).

    3. Number in party/medical situation.

    4. Signal devices available.

e. If no radio, a ground-to-air signal may be your only means to effect recovery.

2. SITE SELECTION The principle consideration for pickup is where it will take place. A linkup with recovery forces will not happen in a vacuum. Your site must be carefully selected and well planned out to control any enemy situation that may occur.

a. Locate area for landing pickup, if practical (approximately 150 feet in diameter, free of obstructions, flat and level).
b. Assess evidence of human activity at/near the site (in combat).
c. Locate several concealment sites around area (in combat).
d. Plan several tactical entry and exit routes (in combat).

3. SITE PREPARATION   Once a site has been selected you must prepare for both pickup and for failed pickup.

a. Pack and secure all equipment.
b. Prepare signaling devices (use as directed or as briefed).
c. Mentally review recovery methods (aircraft, ground, boat, etc.).
d. Plan egress routes in case of failed recovery.

4. RECOVERY PROCEDURES   When the actual recovery is taking place, it will be easy to let your excitement overcome caution. Remember that the recovery team will probably be on edge because of the danger of their mission. It would be very easy to be mistaken for the enemy if you are not careful. Every effort must be made to make the process of identifying you as an evader as easy as possible.

Figure IV–1. Rescue Strap

1 PULL DOWN VELCRO FASTENER

2 PULL OUT STRAP, PLACE LOOP OVER HEAD AND UNDER ARMPITS

3 FOLD DOWN SEAT

4 MOUNT SEAT AND TIGHTEN STRAP

5 GRASP CABLE AND SIGNAL WHEN READY

6 FOLD ARMS AROUND PENETRATOR— KEEP HEAD DOWN

Figure IV-2. Forest Penetrator

a. Assist recovery force in identifying your position.
b. Stay concealed until recovery is imminent (in combat).
c. For a landing/ground recovery—
    1. Assume a nonthreatening posture.
    2. Secure weapons and avoid quick movement.

Figure IV–3. Fixed Loop

3. DO NOT approach recovery vehicle until instructed.
4. Beware of rotors/propellers when approaching recovery vehicle, especially on sloping or uneven terrain. Secure loose equipment that could be caught in rotors/propellers.

d. For hoist recovery devices (FIGURES IV-1 AND IV-2)—

1. Use eye protection, if available (glasses or helmet visor).
2. Allow metal on device to contact the surface before touching to avoid injury from static discharge.
3. Sit or kneel for stability while donning device.
4. Put safety strap under armpits.
5. Ensure cable is in front of you.
6. Keep hands clear of all hardware and connectors.
7. DO NOT become entangled in cable.
8. Use a thumbs up, vigorous cable shake, or radio call to signal you are ready.
9. Drag feet on the ground to decrease oscillation.
10. DO NOT assist during hoist or when pulled into the rescue vehicle. Follow crew member instructions.

e. For non-hoist recovery (rope or unfamiliar equipment)—

1. Create a "fixed loop" big enough to place under armpits (FIGURE IV-3).
2. Follow the procedures in item d above.

CHAPTER V

MEDICAL

WARNING: These emergency medical procedures are for survival situations. Obtain professional medical treatment as soon as possible.

1. IMMEDIATE FIRST AID ACTIONS

Remember the ABCs of Emergency Care:

A	Airway
B	Breathing
C	Circulation

a. Determine responsiveness as follows:

1. If unconscious, arouse by shaking gently and shouting.
2. If no response—
   - Keep head and neck aligned with body.
   - Roll victims onto their backs.
   - Open the airway by lifting the chin (**Figure V-1**).
   - Look, listen, and feel for air exchange.
3. If victim is not breathing—
   - Check for a clear airway; remove any blockage.
   - Cover victim's mouth with your own.
   - Pinch victim's nostrils closed.
   - Fill victim's lungs with two slow breaths.
   - If breaths are blocked, reposition airway; try again.

Figure V-1. Chin Lift

- If breaths still blocked, give five abdominal thrusts:
    - *Straddle the victim.*
    - *Place a fist between breastbone and belly button.*
    - *Thrust upward to expel air from stomach.*
- Sweep with finger to clear mouth.
- Try two slow breaths again.
- If the airway is still blocked, continue previous steps in item 3 until successful or exhausted.
- With open airway, start mouth to mouth breathing:
    - *Give one breath every five seconds.*
    - *Check for chest rise each time.*

4. If victim is unconscious, but breathing—
    - Keep head and neck aligned with body.
    - Roll victim on side (drains the mouth and prevents the tongue from blocking airway).

5. If breathing difficulty is caused by chest trauma, refer to page 47, item d. Treat chest injuries.

CAUTION: DO NOT remove an impaled object unless it interferes with the airway. You may cause more tissue damage and increase bleeding. For travel, you may shorten and secure the object.

b. Control bleeding as follows:
1. Apply a pressure dressing (FIGURE **V-2**).
2. If STILL bleeding—

WOUND

DRESSING

ATTACHED BANDAGES

PRESSURE APPLIED TO WOUND WITH BANDAGES ATTACHED TO DRESSING

ADDITIONAL PRESSURE APPLIED TO WOUND WITH HAND

ADDITIONAL PRESSURE APPLIED TO WOUND WITH PAD (RAG) FIRMLY SECURED WITH CRAVAT OR OTHER STRIP OF MATERIAL

Figure V-2. Application of a Pressure Dressing

- Use direct pressure over the wound.
- Elevate the wounded area above the heart.
3. If STILL bleeding—
   - Use a pressure point between the injury and the heart (Figure V-3).
   - Maintain pressure for six to ten minutes before checking to see if bleeding has stopped.
4. If a limb wound is STILL bleeding—

   CAUTION: Use of a tourniquet is a LAST RESORT measure. Use ONLY when severe, uncontrolled

Figure V-3. Pressure Points

1. Wrap a wide band around the injured limb. Tie with a square knot.

SQUARE KNOT

2. Pass a stick, bayonet, or scabbard through the tourniquet knot.

3. Tighten tourniquet by turning stick just enough to stop arterial bleeding.

4. Bind free end of the stick to keep tourniquet from unwinding.

Figure V-4. Application of a Tourniquet

bleeding will cause loss of life. Recognize that long-term use of a tourniquet may cause loss of limb.

- Apply tourniquet (TK) band just above bleeding site on limb. A band at least 3 inches (7.5 cm) or wider is best.
- Follow steps illustrated in Figure V-4.

- Use a stick at least 6 inches (15 cm) long.
- Tighten only enough to stop arterial bleeding.
- Mark a TK on the forehead with the time applied.
- DO NOT cover the tourniquet.

CAUTION: The following directions apply ONLY in survival situations where rescue is UNLIKELY and NO medical aid is available.

- If rescue or medical aid is not available for over two hours, an attempt to SLOWLY loosen the tourniquet may be made twenty minutes after application. Before loosening—
    Ensure pressure dressing is in place.
    Ensure bleeding has stopped.
    Loosen tourniquet SLOWLY to restore circulation.
    Leave loosened tourniquet in position in case bleeding resumes.

c. Treat shock. (Shock is difficult to identify or treat under field conditions. It may be present with or without visible injury.)
   1. Identify by one or more of the following:
      - Pale, cool, and sweaty skin.
      - Fast breathing and a weak, fast pulse.
      - Anxiety or mental confusion.
      - Decreased urine output.
   2. Maintain circulation.
   3. Treat underlying injury.
   4. Maintain normal body temperature.
      - Remove wet clothing.
      - Give warm fluids.
          DO NOT give fluids to an unconscious victim.
          DO NOT give fluids if they cause victim to gag.
      - Insulate from ground.
      - Shelter from the elements.
   5. Place conscious victim on back.

6. Place very weak or unconscious victim on side; this will—
   - Allow mouth to drain.
   - Prevent tongue from blocking airway.

d. Treat chest injuries.

1. Sucking chest wound. This occurs when the chest cavity is breached and air is being pulled in through the wound by the same action of the diaphragm that fills the lungs. The air coming in through the wound, however, will not be going into the lungs. As the amount of trapped air increases, pressure builds up in the chest. The lung can collapse on that side and can push the other organs in the center of the chest, such as the heart and the major blood vessels and airways, toward the other side of the chest. The shift can cause the other lung to become compressed and can affect the flow of blood returning to the heart.
   - Immediately seal wound with hand or airtight material.
   - Tape airtight material over wound on three sides only (Figure V-5) to allow air to escape from the wound but not to enter.
   - Monitor breathing and check dressing.
   - Lift untaped side of dressing as victim exhales to allow trapped air to escape, as necessary.
2. Flail chest. Results from blunt trauma when three or more ribs are broken in two or more places. The flail segment is the broken area that moves in a direction opposite to the rest of chest during breathing.
   - Stabilize the flail segment as follows:
       Place rolled-up clothing or bulky pad over site.
       Tape pad to site.
       DO NOT wrap tape around chest. This could restrict breathing.

Figure V-5. Sucking Chest Wound Dressing

- Have victim keep segment still with hand pressure.
- Roll victim onto side of flail segment injury (as other injuries allow).
3. Fractured ribs.
   - Encourage deep breathing (painful, but necessary to prevent the possible development of pneumonia).
   - DO NOT constrict breathing by taping ribs.

e. Treat fractures, sprains, and dislocations.
1. Control bleeding.
2. Remove watches, jewelry, and constrictive clothing.
3. If fracture penetrates the skin—
   - Clean wound by gentle irrigation with clean water.
   - Apply dressing over wound.
4. Position limb as normally as possible.

5. Splint in position found (if unable to straighten limb).
6. Improvise a splint with available materials:
   - Sticks or straight, stiff materials from equipment.
   - Body parts (for example, opposite leg, arm-to-chest).
7. Attach with strips of cloth, parachute cord, etc.
8. Keep the fractured bones from moving by immobilizing the joints on both sides of the fracture. If fracture is in a joint, immobilize the bones on both sides of the joint.

CAUTION: Splint fingers in a slightly flexed position, NOT in straight position. Hand should look like it is grasping an apple.

9. Use RICES treatment for seventy-two hours.

R	Rest
I	Ice
C	Compression
E	Elevation
S	Stabilization

10. Apply cold to acute injuries.
11. Use fifteen- to twenty-minute periods of cold application.
    - DO NOT use continuous cold therapy.
    - Repeat three to four times per day.
    - Avoid cooling that can cause frostbite or hypothermia.
12. Wrap with a compression bandage after cold therapy.
13. Elevate injured area above heart level to reduce swelling.
14. Check periodically for a pulse beyond the injury site.

15. Loosen bandage or reapply splint if no pulse is felt or if swelling occurs because bandage is too tight.

2. COMMON INJURIES AND ILLNESSES

a. Burns.
1. Cool the burned area with water.
   - Use immersion or cool compresses.
   - Avoid aggressive cooling with ice or frigid water.
2. Remove watches, jewelry, constrictive clothing.
3. DO NOT remove embedded, charred material that will cause burned areas to bleed.
4. Cover with sterile dressings.
5. DO NOT use lotion or grease.
6. Avoid moving or rubbing the burned part.
7. Drink extra water to compensate for increased fluid loss from burns. (Add ¼ teaspoon of salt [if available] to each quart of water.)
8. Change dressings when soaked or dirty.

b. Eye injuries.
1. Sun/snow blindness (gritty, burning sensation, and possible reduction in vision caused by sun exposure).
   - Prevent with improvised goggles. (See Chapter VI, page 63, Figure VI-2.)
   - Treat by patching affected eye(s).
     Check after twelve hours.
     Replace patch for another twelve hours if not healed.
   - Use cool compresses to reduce pain.
2. Foreign body in eye.
   - Irrigate with clean water from the inside to the outside corner of the eye.
   - If foreign body is not removed by irrigation, improvise a small swab. Moisten and wipe gently over the affected area.

- If foreign body is STILL not removed, patch eye for twenty-four hours and then reattempt removal using previous steps.

c. Heat injury.

1. Heat cramps (cramps in legs or abdomen).
   - Rest.
   - Drink water. Add ¼ teaspoon of salt per quart.
2. Heat exhaustion (pale, sweating, moist, cool skin).
   - Rest in shade.
   - Drink water.
   - Protect from further heat exposure.
3. Heatstroke (victim disoriented or unconscious, skin is hot and flushed [sweating may or may not occur], fast pulse).

   CAUTION: Handle heatstroke victim gently. Shock, seizures, and cardiac arrest can occur.

   - Cool as rapidly as possible (saturate clothing with water and fan the victim). Remember to cool the groin and armpit areas. (Avoid overcooling.)
   - Maintain airway, breathing, and circulation.

d. Cold injuries:

1. Frostnip and frostbite—
   - Are progressive injuries.
     Ears, nose, fingers, and toes are affected first.
     Areas will feel cold and may tingle, leading to—
     Numbness that progresses to—
     Waxy appearance with stiff skin that cannot glide freely over a joint.
   - Frostnipped areas rewarm with body heat. If body heat WILL NOT rewarm area in fifteen to twenty minutes, then frostbite is present.
   - Frostbitten areas are deeply frozen and require medical treatment.

CAUTION: In frostbite, repeated freezing and thawing causes severe pain and increases damage to the tissue. DO NOT rub frozen tissue. DO NOT thaw frozen tissue.

2. Hypothermia—
   * Is a progressive injury.
        Intense shivering with impaired ability to perform complex tasks leads to—
        Violent shivering, difficulty speaking, sluggish thinking, which proceed to—
        Muscular rigidity with blue, puffy skin; jerk movements, leading to—
        Coma, respiratory and cardiac failure.
   * Protect victim from the environment as follows:
        Remove wet clothing.
        Put on dry clothing (if available).
        Prevent further heat loss.
        Cover top of head.
        Insulate from above and below.
        Warm with blankets, sleeping bags, or shelter.
        Warm central areas before extremities.
        Place heat packs in groin, armpits, and around neck.
        Avoid causing burns to skin.

CAUTION: Handle hypothermia victim gently. Avoid overly rapid rewarming, which may cause cardiac arrest. Rewarming of victim with skin-to-skin contact by volunteer(s) inside of a sleeping bag is a survival technique but can cause internal temperatures of all to drop.

e. Skin tissue damage.
   1. Immersion injuries. Skin becomes wrinkled as in dishpan hands.
      * Avoid walking on affected feet.

- Pat dry; DO NOT rub. Skin tissue will be sensitive.
- Dry socks and shoes. Keep feet protected.
- Loosen boots, cuffs, etc., to improve circulation.
- Keep area dry, warm, and open to air.
- DO NOT apply creams or ointments.

2. Saltwater sores.
   - Change body positions frequently.
   - Keep sores dry.
   - Use antiseptic (if available).
   - DO NOT open or squeeze sores.

f. Snakebite.

CAUTION: This snakebite treatment recommendation is for situations where medical aid and specialized equipment are not available.

1. Nonpoisonous. Clean and bandage wound.
2. Poisonous.
   - Remove constricting items.
   - Minimize activity.
   - DO NOT cut the bite site; DO NOT use your mouth to create suction.
   - Clean bite with soap and water; cover with a dressing.
   - Overwrap the bite site with a tight (elastic) bandage (FIGURE V-6). The intent is to slow capillary and venous blood flow but not arterial flow. Check for pulse below the overwrap.
   - Splint bitten extremity to prevent motion.
   - Treat for shock (page 46).
   - Position extremity below level of heart.
   - Construct shelter if necessary (let the victim rest).
   - For conscious victims, force fluids.

Figure V-6. Compression Bandage for Snake Bite

g. Marine life.

1. Stings.
   - Flush wound with salt water (freshwater stimulates toxin release).
   - Remove jewelry and watches.
   - Remove tentacles and gently scrape or shave skin.
   - Apply a steroid cream (if available).
   - DO NOT rub area with sand.
   - Treat for shock; artificial respiration may be required (page 41).
   - DO NOT use urine to flush or treat wounds.
2. Punctures.
   - Immerse affected part in hot water or apply hot compresses for thirty to sixty minutes (as hot as victim can tolerate).
   - Cover with clean dressing.
   - Treat for shock as needed.

h. Skin irritants (includes poison oak and poison ivy).

1. Wash with large amounts of water. Use soap (if available).
2. Keep covered to prevent scratching.

i. Infection.

1. Keep wound clean.
2. Use iodine tablet solution or diluted Betadine to prevent or treat infection.
3. Change bandages as needed.

j. Dysentery and diarrhea.

1. Drink extra water.
2. Use a liquid diet.
3. Eat charcoal. Make a paste by mixing fine charcoal particles with water. (It may relieve symptoms by absorbing toxins.)

k. Constipation (can be expected in survival situations).
1. DO NOT take laxatives.
2. Exercise.
3. Drink extra water.

3. PLANT MEDICINE

a. Tannin.
1. Medical uses. Burns, diarrhea, dysentery, skin problems, and parasites. Tannin solution prevents infection and aids healing.
2. Sources. Found in the outer bark of all trees, acorns, banana plants, common plantain, strawberry leaves, and blackberry stems.
3. Preparation.
   - Place crushed outer bark, acorns, or leaves in water.
   - Leach out the tannin by soaking or boiling.
     Increase tannin content by longer soaking time.
     Replace depleted material with fresh bark/
       plants.
4. Treatments.
   - Burns.
     Moisten bandage with cooled tannin tea.
     Apply compress to burned area.
     Pour cooled tea on burned areas to ease pain.
   - Diarrhea, dysentery, and worms. Drink strong tea solution (may promote voiding of worms).
   - Skin problems (dry rashes and fungal infections). Apply cool compresses or soak affected part to relieve itching and promote healing.
   - Lice and insect bites. Wash affected areas with tea to ease itching.

b. Salicin/salicylic acid.
1. Medical uses. Aches, colds, fever, inflammation,

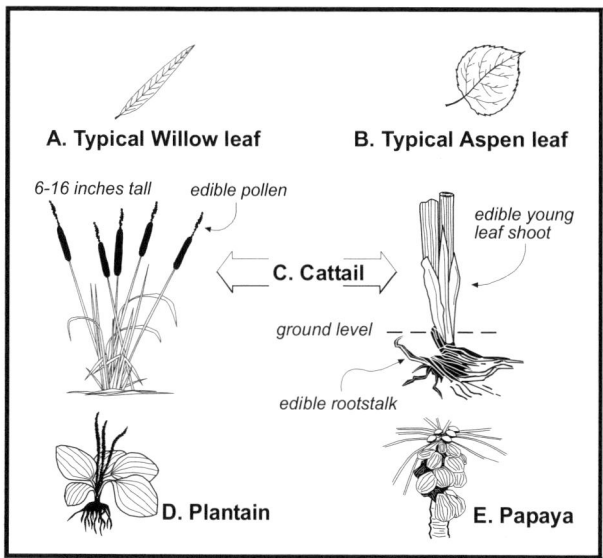

A. Typical Willow leaf

B. Typical Aspen leaf

6-16 inches tall   edible pollen

edible young leaf shoot

C. Cattail

ground level

edible rootstalk

D. Plantain

E. Papaya

Figure V-7. Useful Plants

pain, sprains, and sore throat (aspirin-like qualities).
2. Sources. Willow and aspen trees (**Figure V-7**).
3. Preparation.
   - Gather twigs, buds, or cambium layer (soft, moist layer between the outer bark and the wood) of willow or aspen.
   - Prepare tea as described in item 3, Preparation, on page 56.
   - Make poultice.
     Crush the plant or stems.
     Make a pulpy mass.
4. Treatments.
   - Chew on twigs, buds, or cambium for symptom relief.
   - Drink tea for colds and sore throat.

- Use warm, moist poultice for aches and sprains.
  Apply pulpy mass over injury.
  Hold in place with a dressing.

c. Common plantain.
1. Medical uses. Itching, wounds, abrasions, stings, diarrhea, and dysentery.
2. Source. There are over 200 plantain species with similar medicinal properties. The common plantain is shown in Figure V-7.
3. Preparation.
   - Brew tea from seeds.
   - Brew tea from leaves.
   - Make poultice of leaves.
4. Treatments.
   - Drink tea made from seeds for diarrhea or dysentery.
   - Drink tea made from leaves for vitamin and minerals.
   - Use poultice to treat cuts, sores, burns, and stings.

d. Papain.
1. Medical uses. Digestive aid, meat tenderizer, and a food source.
2. Source. Fruit of the papaya tree (Figure V-7).
3. Preparation.
   - Make cuts in unripe fruit.
   - Gather milky white sap for its papain content.
   - Avoid getting sap in eyes or wounds.
4. Treatments.
   - Use sap to tenderize tough meat.
   - Eat ripe fruit for food, vitamins, and minerals.

e. Common Cattail.
1. Medical uses. Wounds, sores, boils, inflammations, burns, and an excellent food source.

2. Source. Cattail plant found in marshes (Figure V-7).
   3. Preparation.
      • Pound roots into a pulpy mass for a poultice.
      • Cook and eat green bloom spikes.
      • Collect yellow pollen for flour substitute.
      • Peel and eat tender shoots (raw or cooked).
   4. Treatments.
      • Apply poultice to affected area.
      • Use plant for food, vitamins, and minerals.

4. HEALTH AND HYGIENE

a. Stay clean (daily regimen).
   1. Minimize infection by washing. (Use white ashes, sand, or loamy soil as soap substitutes.)
   2. Comb and clean debris from hair.
   3. Cleanse mouth and brush teeth.
      • Use hardwood twig as toothbrush (fray it by chewing on one end then use as brush).
      • Use single strand of an inner core string from parachute cord for dental floss.
      • Use clean finger to stimulate gum tissues by rubbing.
      • Gargle with salt water to help prevent sore throat and aid in cleaning teeth and gums.
   4. Clean and protect feet.
      • Change and wash socks.
      • Wash, dry, and massage.
      • Check frequently for blisters and red areas.
      • Use adhesive tape/moleskin to prevent damage.

b. Exercise daily.
c. Prevent and control parasites.
   1. Check body for lice, fleas, ticks, etc.
      • Check body regularly.
      • Pick off insects and eggs (DO NOT crush).

2. Wash clothing and use repellents.
3. Use smoke to fumigate clothing and equipment.

5. RULES FOR AVOIDING ILLNESS

a. *Purify all water obtained from natural sources by using iodine tablets, bleach, or boiling for five minutes.*
b. *Locate latrines 200 feet from water and away from shelter.*
c. *Wash hands before preparing food or water.*
d. *Clean all eating utensils after each meal.*
e. *Prevent insect bites by using repellent, netting, and clothing.*
f. *Dry wet clothing as soon as possible.*
g. *Eat varied diet.*
h. *Try to get seven to eight hours sleep per day.*

CHAPTER VI

PERSONAL PROTECTION

1. PRIORITIES

a. Evaluate available resources and situation, then accomplish individual tasks accordingly.
b. First twenty-four hours, in order of situational needs—
   1. Construct survival shelter according to selection criteria.
   2. Procure water.
   3. Establish multiple survival signals.
   4. Build fire.

c. Second twenty-four hours, in order of situational needs—
   1. Construct necessary tools and weapons.
   2. Procure food.

2. CARE AND USE OF CLOTHING

a. Never discard clothing.
b. Wear loose and layered clothing.
   1. Tight clothing restricts body temperature–regulating blood flow.
   2. Layers create more dead air space.

c. Keep entire body covered to prevent sunburn and dehydration in hot climates. When fully clothed, the majority of body heat escapes through the head and neck areas.

d. Avoid overheating.
1. Remove layers of clothing before strenuous activities.
2. Use a hat to regulate body heat.
3. Wear a hat when in direct sunlight (in hot environment).

e. Dampen clothing when on the ocean in hot weather.
1. Use salt water, NOT drinking water.
2. Dry clothing before dark to prevent hypothermia.

f. Keep clothing dry to maintain its insulation qualities (dry damp clothing in the sun or by a fire).
g. If you fall into the water in the winter—
1. Build fire.
2. Remove wet clothing and rewarm by fire.
3. Finish drying clothing by fire.

h. If no fire is available—
1. Remove clothing and get into sleeping bag (if available).
2. Allow wet clothes to freeze.
3. Break ice out of clothing.

i. Keep clothing clean (dirt reduces its insulation qualities). Examine clothing frequently for damage.
1. DO NOT sit or lie directly on the ground.
2. Wash clothing whenever possible.
3. Repair when necessary by using—
   - Needle and thread.
   - Safety pins.
   - Tape.

j. Improvised foot protection (FIGURE VI-1).
1. Cut two to four layers of cloth into a 30-inch square.
2. Fold into a triangle.

Figure VI-1. Improvised Footwear

Figure VI-2. Sun and Snow Goggles

3. Center foot on triangle with toes toward corner.
4. Fold front over the toes.
5. Fold side corners, one at a time, over the instep.
6. Secure by rope, vines, tape, etc., or tuck into other layers of material.

3. OTHER PROTECTIVE EQUIPMENT

a. Sleeping bag.
1. Fluff before use, especially at foot of bag.
2. Air and dry daily to remove body moisture.
3. Improvise with available material, dry grass, leaves, dry moss, etc.

b. Sun and snow goggles (FIGURE VI-2).
1. Wear in bright sun or snow conditions.
2. Improvise by cutting small horizontal slits in webbing, bark, or similar materials.

Figure VI-3. Gaiters

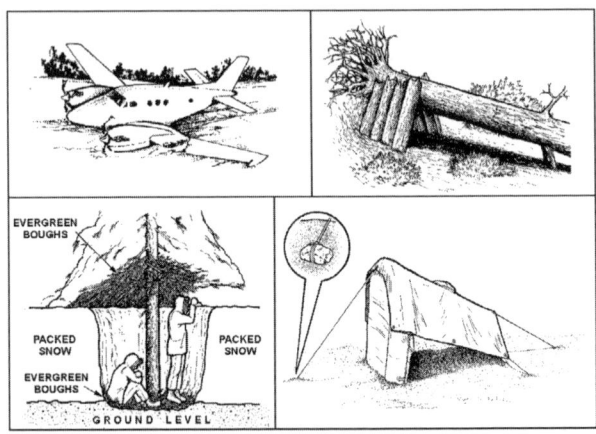

EVERGREEN
BOUGHS

PACKED
SNOW

PACKED
SNOW

EVERGREEN
BOUGHS

GROUND LEVEL

Figure VI-4. Immediate Shelters

c. Gaiters (Figure VI-3). *Used to protect from sand, snow, insects, and scratches (wrap material around lower leg and top of boots).*

4. SHELTERS Evasion considerations apply.

a. Site selection.
1. Near signal and recovery site.
2. Available food and water.
3. Avoid natural hazards:
   • Dead standing trees.

- Drainage and dry riverbeds except in combat areas.
- Avalanche areas.
4. Location large and level enough to lie down in.

b. Types.

1. Immediate shelters. Find shelter needing minimal improvements (**Figure VI-4**).
2. General shelter. Temperate climates require any shelter that gives protection from wind and rain.
3. Thermal A-frame, snow trench, snow cave. (**Figures VI-5** through **VI-7**). Cold climates require an enclosed, insulated shelter.
   - Snow is the most abundant insulating material.
   - Air vent is required to prevent carbon monoxide poisoning when using an open flame inside enclosed shelters.

NOTE: As a general rule, unless you can see your breath, your snow shelter is too warm and should be cooled down to preclude melting and dripping.

Figure VI-5. Thermal A-Frame

Figure VI-6. Snow Trench

Figure VI-7. Snow Cave

4. Shade shelter. Hot climates require a shade shelter to protect from ultraviolet rays (**Figure VI-8**).
   - To reduce the surface temperature, the shelter floor should be elevated or dug down (approximately 18 inches).
   - For thermal protection, a minimum of two layers of material suspended 12 to 18 inches above the head is required. White is the best color to reflect heat (innermost layer should be of darker material).
5. Elevated platform shelter (**Figure VI-9**). Tropical/wet climates require enclosed, elevated shelter for protection from dampness and insects.

c. Shelter construction.
1. Have entrance 45 to 90 degrees from prevailing wind.
2. Cover with available material.
   - If natural materials are used, arrange them in layers starting at the bottom with each layer overlapping the previous one. See **Figure VI-10** for an example.

Figure VI-8. Poncho/Parachute Shade Shelter

Figure VI-9. Elevated Platform Shelter

Figure VI-10. Shingle Method

- If using porous material like parachute, blankets, etc.—

    Stretch as tight as possible.
    Use a 40 to 60 degree slope.
    Use additional layers in heavy rain.

d. Shelter construction materials:

1. Raft and raft parts.
2. Vehicle or aircraft parts.
3. Blankets, poncho, or parachute material.
4. Sheet of plastic or plastic bag.
5. Bark peeled off dead trees.
6. Boughs, broad leaves, dry moss.
7. Grass and sod.
8. Snow.
9. Sand and rocks.

e. Bed construction. Construct a bed to protect from cold, damp ground using—
    1. Raft or foam rubber from vehicle seats.
    2. Boughs, leaves, or dry moss.

5. FIRES

> **CAUTION:** Weigh hazards and risks of detection against the need for a fire.

a. Evasion considerations:
    1. Use trees or other sources to dissipate smoke.
    2. Use the fire pit to lower your heat signature.
    3. Use fires at dusk, dawn, or during inclement weather.
    4. Use fires at times when the local populace is cooking.
    5. Cut out sod and replace over fire remnants to hide sign.

b. Fire building. The three essential elements for starting a fire are heat, fuel, and oxygen.
    1. Heat sources:
       • Matches or lighter.
       • Flint and steel (experiment with various rocks and metals until a good spark is produced).
       • Sparks from batteries.
       • Concentrated sunlight (use magnifying glass or flashlight reflectors).
       • Pyrotechnics, such as flares (last resort), etc.
       • Friction method **(Figure VI-11).** Without prior training, this method is difficult to master and requires a lot of time to build the device.

NOTE: If possible, carry a fire-starting device with you.

Figure VI-11. Friction Method

2. Fuel is divided into three categories: tinder, kindling, and fuel. (Gather large amounts of each category before igniting the fire.)

   • **Tinder.** Tinder must be very finely shaved or shredded to provide a low combustion point and fluffed to allow oxygen to flow through. (To get tinder to burn hotter and longer, saturate with Vaseline, Chapstick, insect repellent, aircraft fuel, etc.) Examples of tinder include—

   Cotton.
   Candle (shred the wick, not the wax).
   Plastic spoon, fork, or knife.
   Foam rubber.
   Dry bark.
   Dry grasses.
   Gunpowder.
   Pitch.
   Petroleum products.

   • **Kindling.** Kindling must be small enough to

ignite from the small flame of the tinder. Gradually add larger kindling until arriving at the size of fuel to burn.

- **Fuel**. Examples of fuel include—

  Dry hardwood (removing bark reduces smoke).
  Bamboo (open chambers to prevent explosion).
  Dry dung.

c. Types. Fires are built to meet specific needs or uses.

1. Tepee fire (**FIGURE VI-12**). Use the tepee fire to produce a concentrated heat source for cooking, lighting, or signaling.
2. Log cabin fire (**FIGURE VI-13**). Use the log cabin fire to produce large amounts of light and heat, to dry out wet wood, and provide coals for cooking, etc.

Figure VI-12. Tepee Fire

Figure VI-13. Log Cabin or Pyramid Fires

3. Sod fire and reflector (**Figure VI-14**). Use fire reflectors to get the most warmth from a fire. Build fires against rocks or logs.

   CAUTION: DO NOT use porous rocks or riverbed rock—they may explode when heated.

4. Dakota fire hole (**Figure VI-15**). Use the Dakota fire hole for high winds or evasion situations.
5. Improvised stoves (**Figure VI-16**). These are very efficient.

6. WEAPONS Weapons serve a dual purpose. You use them to obtain and prepare food and to provide self defense. A weapon can also give you a feeling of security and provide you with the ability to hunt on the move. Weapons can be classified by the type of attacking action they require. In a survival situation ease of manufacture is also an important consideration.

a. Bludgeoning weapons. The simplest type of contact weapon is a bludgeon. A bludgeon is any weapon that you swing at your target.
1. A simple club can be made from a stout staff or tree branch.
2. A weighted club can be made by securely attaching something to the end of a simple club.
3. A flail is made by attaching a weighted object to the end of a simple club with a short length of strong, flexible lashing material.

b. Thrusting weapons. Thrusting weapons are those that you use by thrusting but which are long enough to be useful at extended range. This can be either a one- or two-handed weapon. The most useful and easiest to manufacture in a field expedient manner are spears. Although spears can be thrown,

Figure VI-14. Sod Fire and Reflector

Figure VI-15. Dakota Fire Hole

Figure VI-16. Improvised Stove

the most effective way to use them is to hold them in both hands and thrust toward your target.

1. A simple spear can be made by sharpening the end of a suitable stick and, if possible, hardening the end in a fire.
2. A spear can be made more effective by the use of a spearhead of metal, bone, or even glass.

c. Close contact weapons. Close contact weapons are those that are most useful when at extremely close range. A fixed-blade knife is the most useful type of close contact weapon because it is purposefully built for the actions necessary for fighting at this range.

d. Projectile weapons. The most useful projectile weapons are the types that you may have with you, such as a rifle or a pistol. Useful field expedient projectile weapons take more time and expertise to manufacture.

1. A throwing stick similar to the Australian aboriginal boomerang can be easily made and is useful against small game.
2. For capturing running game or low-flying fowl, a bola can be made by tying three cords together and attaching a weight to the end of each.

CHAPTER VII

WATER

1. WATER REQUIREMENTS   Drink extra water. Minimum two quarts per day to maintain fluid level. Exertion, heat, injury, or an illness increases water loss.

NOTE: Pale yellow urine indicates adequate hydration.

2. WATER PROCUREMENT
a. DO NOT drink—
1. Urine.
2. Fish juices.
3. Blood.
4. Seawater.
5. Alcohol.
6. Melted water from new sea ice.

b. Water sources:
1. Surface water (streams, lakes, and springs).
2. Precipitation (rain, snow, dew, sleet) (FIGURE VII-1).
3. Subsurface (wells and cisterns).
4. Groundwater (when no surface water is available) (FIGURE VII-2).
   • Abundance of lush green vegetation.
   • Drainages and low-lying areas.
   • "V" intersecting game trails often point to water.
   • Presence of swarming insects indicates water is near.

- Bird flight in the early morning or late afternoon might indicate the direction to water.
5. Snow or ice.
  - DO NOT eat ice or snow.
    Lowers body temperature.

Figure VII-1. Water Procurement

Figure VII-2. Water Indicators

Figure VII-3. Water Generator

> *Induces dehydration.*
> *Causes minor cold injury to lips and mouth.*

- Melt with fire.
  > *Stir frequently to prevent damaging container.*
  > *Speed the process by adding hot rocks or water.*
- Melt with body heat.
  > *Use waterproof container.*
  > *Place between layers of clothing.*
  > *DO NOT place next to the skin.*
- Use a water generator (**Figure VII-3**).

6. Open seas.
   - Water available in survival kits.
   - Precipitation.
     > *Drink as much as possible.*
     > *Catch rain in spray shields and life raft covers.*
     > *Collect dew off raft.*
   - Old sea ice or icebergs (**Table VII-1**).

7. Tropical areas.
   - All open sources previously mentioned.
   - Vegetation.
     > *Plants with hollow sections can collect moisture.*

OLD SEA ICE	NEW SEA ICE
Bluish or blackish	Milky or grey
Shatters easily	Does not break easily
Rounded corners	Sharp edges
Tastes relatively salt-free	Tastes extremely salty

Table VII-1. Sea Ice

Figure VII-4. Leaning Tree

Leaning Tree. Cloth absorbs rain running down tree and drips into container (FIGURE VII-4).

Banana plants.

Water trees (avoid milky sap).

Tap before dark. Let sap stop running and harden during the daytime.

Produce most water at night.

For evasion situations, bore into the roots and collect water.

Vines (FIGURE VII-5A).

Cut bark (DO NOT use milky sap).

If juice is clear and water-like, cut as large a piece of vine as possible (cut the top first).

Pour into hand to check smell, color, and taste to determine if drinkable.

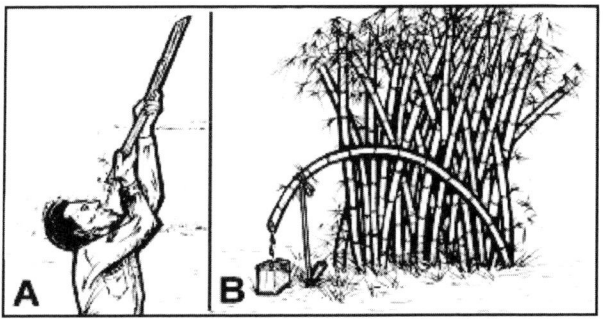

Figure VII-5 A and B. Water Vines and Green Bamboo

> DO NOT touch vine to lips.
> When water flow stops, cut off 6 inches of opposite end; water will flow again.
> Old bamboo.
> Shake and listen for water.
> Bore hole at bottom of section to obtain water.
> Cut out entire section to carry with you.
> Filter and purify.
> Green bamboo (FIGURE VII-5B).
> Beach well. Along the coast, obtain water by digging a beach well (FIGURE VII-6).

CAUTION: Liquid contained in green coconuts (ripe coconuts may cause diarrhea).

8. Dry areas.
   - Solar still (FIGURE VII-7).
   - Vegetation bag (FIGURE VII-8).
   - Transpiration bag (FIGURE VII-9).
     > Water bag must be clear.
     > Water will taste like the plant smells.
   - Seepage basin (FIGURE VII-10).

CAUTION: DO NOT use poisonous/toxic plants in vegetation/transpiration bags.

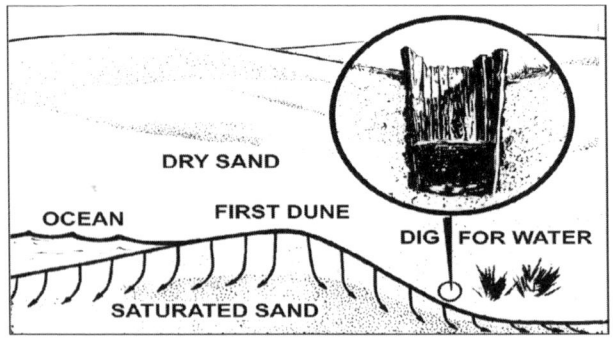

DRY SAND

OCEAN **FIRST DUNE**

DIG FOR WATER

SATURATED SAND

Figure VII-6. Beach Well

DRINKING TUBE

DIRT TO ANCHOR PLASTIC SHEET

APRX 3 FT

APRX 15 IN

CLEAR PLASTIC SHEET

ROCK WEIGHT

DIG OUT TO PLACE MOISTURE PRODUCERS

CONTAINER

Figure VII-7. Solar Still

3. WATER PREPARATION AND STORAGE

a. Filtration. Filter through porous material (sand/charcoal).
b. Purification.
　　1. Water from live plants requires no further
　　　　treatment.
　　2. Purify all other water.
　　　　• Boil at least one minute.
　　　　• Pour from one container to another to improve
　　　　　taste to aerate.
　　　　• Water purification tablets. Follow instructions on
　　　　　package.

Figure VII-8. Vegetation Bag

Figure VII-9. Transpiration Bag

Figure VII-10. Seepage Basin

c. Potable Water.
1. If water cannot be purified, obtain water from a clear, cold, clean, and fast-running source (if possible).
2. Put in clear container and expose to the sun's ultraviolet rays to kill bacteria.

d. Storage. To prevent contamination, use a clean, covered or sealed container.
1. Trash bag.
2. Prophylactic.
3. Section of bamboo.
4. Flotation gear.

CHAPTER VIII

FOOD

1. FOOD PROCUREMENT

a. Sources and location.

1. Mammals can be found where—
   - Trails lead to watering, feeding, and bedding areas.
   - Droppings or tracks look fresh.
2. Birds can be found by—
   - Observing the direction of flight in the early morning and late afternoon (leads to feeding, watering, and roosting areas).
   - Listening for bird noises (indication of nesting areas).
3. Fish and other marine life locations (Figure VIII-1).
4. Reptiles and amphibians are found almost worldwide.
5. Insects are found—
   - In dead logs and stumps.
   - At ant and termite mounds.
   - On ponds, lakes, and slow-moving streams.

b. Procurement techniques.

1. Snares—
   - Work while unattended.

1	OVERHANGING BRUSH
2	UNDERCUT
3	POOL FROM BACKWASH
4	FEEDER STREAM
5	BEHIND ROCKS
6	FALLEN TREE

Figure VIII-1. Fishing Locations

Figure VIII-2. Snare Placement

- Location:
    *Trails leading to water, feeding, and bedding
        areas.*
    Mouth of dens (FIGURE VIII-2).

- Construction of simple loop snare.

  Use materials that will not break under the strain of holding an animal.

  Use a figure eight (locking loop) if wire is used (Figure VIII-3).

  Once tightened, the wire locks in place, preventing reopening, and the animal's escape.

  To construct a squirrel pole (Figure VIII-4), use simple loop snares.

  Make noose opening slightly larger than the animal's head (three-finger width for squirrels, fist-sized for rabbits).

Figure VIII-3. Locking Loop

Figure VIII-4. Squirrel Pole

Figure VIII-5. Funneling

- Placement of snares (set as many as possible).
    Avoid disturbing the area.
    Use funneling (natural or improvised) (Figure VIII-5).
2. Noose stick (easier and safer to use than the hands). Twist stick (Figure VIII-6).
    - Insert forked stick into a den until something soft is met.
    - Twist the stick, binding the animal's hide in the fork.
    - Remove the animal from the den.
    - Be ready to kill the animal; it may be dangerous.
3. Hunting and fishing devices. (See Figure VIII-7 for fishing procurement methods.)
    - Club or rock.
    - Spear.
    - Slingshot.
    - Pole, line, and hook.
    - Net.
    - Trap.
4. Precautions:
    - Wear shoes to protect the feet when wading in water.
    - Avoid reaching into dark holes.

Figure VIII-6. Procurement Devices

Figure VIII-7. Procurement Methods

- Kill animals before handling. Animals in distress may attract the enemy.
- DO NOT secure fishing lines to yourself or the raft.
- Kill fish before bringing them into the raft.
- DO NOT eat fish with—
    Spines.
    Unpleasant odor.
    Pale, slimy gills.
    Sunken eyes.

Flabby skin.
Flesh that remains dented when pressed.
- DO NOT eat fish eggs or liver (entrails).
- Avoid all crustaceans above the high tide mark.
- Avoid crustaceans in industrial areas.
- Avoid cone-shaped shells (**Figure VIII-8).**
- Avoid hairy insects; the hairs could cause irritation or infection.
- Avoid poisonous insects, for example:
  Centipedes.
  Scorpions.
  Poisonous spiders.

Cone shell

Warning!
These snails can sting and cause acute pain, swelling, paralysis, blindness, and possible death in a few hours.

Terebra shell

Figure VIII-8. Cone-Shaped Shells of Venomous Snails

- Avoid disease-carrying insects, such as—
  Flies.
  Mosquitoes.
  Ticks.

c. Plant Foods. Before using the following guide, use your evasion chart to identify edible plants:

> **NOTE:** If you cannot positively identify an edible plant and choose to try an unknown plant, these guidelines may help determine edibility.

1. Selection criteria.
   - Before testing for edibility, ensure there are enough plants to make testing worth your time and effort. Each part of a plant (roots, leaves, stems, bark, etc.) requires more than twenty-four hours to test. DO NOT waste time testing a plant that is not abundant.
   - Test only one part of one plant at a time.
   - Remember that eating large portions of plant food on an empty stomach may cause diarrhea, nausea, or cramps. Two good examples are green apples and wild onions. Even after testing food and finding it safe, eat in moderation.
2. Avoid plants with the following characteristics:

> **NOTE:** Using these guidelines in selecting plants for food may eliminate some edible plants; however, these guidelines will help prevent choosing potentially toxic plants.

- Milky sap (dandelion has milky sap but is safe to eat and easily recognizable).
- Spines, fine hairs, and thorns (skin irritants/ contact dermatitis). Prickly pear and thistles are exceptions. Bracken fern fiddleheads also violate this guideline.

- Mushrooms and fungus.
- Umbrella-shaped flowers (hemlock is eliminated).
- Bulbs (only onions smell like onions).
- Grain heads with pink, purplish, or black spurs.
- Beans, bulbs, or seeds inside pods.
- Old or wilted leaves.
- Plants with shiny leaves.
- White and yellow berries. (Aggregate berries such as black and dewberries are always edible; test all others before eating.)
- Almond scent in woody parts and leaves.

d. Test procedures.

CAUTION: Test all parts of the plant for edibility. Some plants have both edible and inedible parts. NEVER ASSUME a part that proved edible when cooked is edible raw; test the part raw before eating. The same part or plant may produce varying reactions in different individuals.

1. Test only one part of a plant at a time.
2. Separate the plant into its basic components (stems, roots, buds, and flowers).
3. Smell the food for strong acid odors. Remember, smell alone does not indicate a plant is edible or inedible.
4. DO NOT eat eight hours before the test and drink only purified water.
5. During the eight hours you abstain from eating, test for contact poisoning by placing a piece of the plant on the inside of your elbow or wrist. The sap or juice should contact the skin. Usually fifteen minutes is enough time to allow for a reaction.
6. During testing, take NOTHING by mouth EXCEPT purified water and the plant you are testing.
7. Select a small portion of a single part and prepare it the way you plan to eat it.

8. Before placing the prepared plant in your mouth, touch a small portion (a pinch) to the outer surface of your lip to test for burning or itching.
9. If after three minutes there is no reaction on your lip, place the plant on your tongue and hold it for fifteen minutes.
10. If there is no reaction, thoroughly chew a pinch and hold it in your mouth for fifteen minutes (DO NOT SWALLOW). If any ill effects occur, rinse out your mouth with water.
11. If nothing abnormal occurs, swallow the food and wait eight hours. If any ill effects occur during this period, induce vomiting and drink a water and charcoal mixture.
12. If no ill effects occur, eat ¼ cup of the same plant prepared the same way. Wait another eight hours. If no ill effects occur, the plant part as prepared is safe for eating.

CAUTION:

1. Ripe tropical fruits should be peeled and eaten raw. Softness, rather than color, is the best indicator of ripeness. Cook unripe fruits and discard seeds and skin.
2. Cook underground portions when possible to reduce bacterial contamination and ease digestion of their generally high starch content.
3. During evasion, you may not be able to cook. Concentrate your efforts on leafy green plants, ripe fruits, and above-ground ripe vegetables not requiring significant preparation.

2. FOOD PREPARATION Animal food gives the greatest food value per pound.

a. Butchering and skinning.
1. Mammals.
   - Remove the skin and save for other uses.
   - One-cut skinning of small game (**Figure VIII-9**).
     Open the abdominal cavity.
     Avoid rupturing the intestines.
     Remove the intestines.
     Save inner organs (heart, liver, and kidneys) and all meaty parts of the skull, brain, tongue, and eyes.
   - Wash when ready to use.
   - If preserving the meat, remove it from the bones.
   - Unused or inedible organs and entrails may be used as bait for other game.
2. Frogs and snakes.
   - Skin.
   - Discard skin, head with 2 inches of body, and internal organs.
3. Fish.
   - Scale (if necessary) and gut fish soon after it is caught.

Figure VIII-9. Small Game Skinning

- Insert knifepoint into anus of fish and cut open the belly.
- Remove entrails.
- Remove gills to prevent spoilage.
4. Birds.
- Gut soon after killing.
- Protect from flies.
- Skin or pluck them.
- Skin scavengers and seabirds.
5. Insects.
- Remove all hard portions such as the legs of grasshoppers or crickets. (The rest is edible.)
- Recommend cooking grasshopper-size insects.

CAUTION: Dead insects spoil rapidly; DO NOT save.

6. Fruits, berries, and most nuts can be eaten raw.

b. Cooking.

CAUTION: To kill parasites, thoroughly cook all wild game, freshwater fish, clams, mussels, snails, crawfish, and scavenger birds. Saltwater fish may be eaten raw.

1. Boiling (most nutritious method of cooking—drink the broth).
- Make metal cooking containers from ration cans.
- Drop heated rocks into containers to boil water or cook food.
2. Baking.
- Wrap in leaves or pack in mud.
- Bury food in dirt under coals of fire.
3. Leaching. Some nuts (acorns) must be leached to remove the bitter taste of tannin. Use one of the following leaching methods:
- First method:

Soaking and pouring the water off.
Crushing and pouring water through. Cold water should be tried first; however, boiling water is sometimes best.
Discarding water.
- Second method:
  Boil, pour off water, and taste the plant.
  If bitter, repeat process until palatable.
4. Roasting.
   - Shake shelled nuts in a container with hot coals.
   - Roast thinly sliced meat and insects over a candle.

3. FOOD PRESERVATION
a. Keeping an animal alive.
b. Refrigerating.
1. Long term.
   - Food buried in snow maintains a temperature of approximately 32 degrees Fahrenheit.
   - Frozen food will not decompose (freeze in meal-size portions).
2. Short term.
   - Food wrapped in waterproof material and placed in a stream remains cool in summer months.
   - Earth below the surface, particularly in shady areas or along streams, is cooler than the surface.
   - Wrap food in absorbent material such as cotton and rewet as the water evaporates.

c. Drying and smoking removes moisture and preserves food.
1. Use salt to improve flavor and promote drying.
2. Cut or pound meat into thin strips.
3. Remove fat.
4. DO NOT use pitch woods such as fir or pine; they produce soot, giving the meat an undesirable taste.

d. Protecting meat from animals and insects.
- 1. Wrapping food.
  - Use clean material.
  - Wrap pieces individually.
  - Ensure all corners of the wrapping are insect-proof.
  - Wrap soft fruits and berries in leaves or moss.
- 2. Hanging meat.
  - Hang meat in the shade.
  - Cover during daylight hours to protect from insects.
- 3. Packing meat on the trail.
  - Wrap before flies appear in the morning.
  - Place meat in fabric or clothing for insulation.
  - Place meat inside the pack for carrying. Soft material acts as insulation, helping keep the meat cool.
  - Carry shellfish, crabs, and shrimp in wet seaweed.

e. DO NOT store food in the shelter; it attracts unwanted animals.

CHAPTER IX

CONTACT WITH THE INDIGENOUS

1. MAKING CONTACT   You should only make contact with any indigenous people if it is absolutely necessary to your survival. It is important to understand the political situation of the area you are operating in. Are they more likely to be friendly or hostile, or will they simply ignore you? Are there certain ethnic groups or subcultures more disposed to help? This will give you insight into what the people of the area may think about your presence and whether they are likely to hurt or help you in your efforts to survive. Once you understand the political context, your actions when dealing with local peoples must be sensitive to their culture. Dealing with an urban or educated populace will be quite different than dealing with primitive farmers. The best advice will always be to accept, respect, and adapt to their ways.

2. MAKE CONTACT CAUTIOUSLY
a. Observe their habits and make a plan.
b. Wait until only one person is near and allow them to approach you if possible.
c. Avoid contact with females.
d. Be friendly; smile as often as you can.

3. BEHAVE APPROPRIATELY

a. Learn local customs and follow them.

1. Accept their hospitality.
2. Avoid taboo areas.
3. Befriend people who approach you.
4. Avoid touching people.
5. Keep your promises.

b. Avoid diseases.

1. Build a separate shelter if possible.
2. Personally prepare your food and drink if you can do so without causing offense.
3. Avoid sexual contact. Not only is this a good idea to avoid disease, but one of the quickest ways to get handed over to the enemy, even by friendly people, is to make someone jealous.

CHAPTER X

INDUCED CONDITIONS

(NUCLEAR, BIOLOGICAL, AND CHEMICAL CONSIDERATIONS)

1. NUCLEAR CONDITIONS

CAUTION: Radiation protection depends on time of exposure, distance from the source, and shielding.

Figure X-1. Immediate Action Shelter

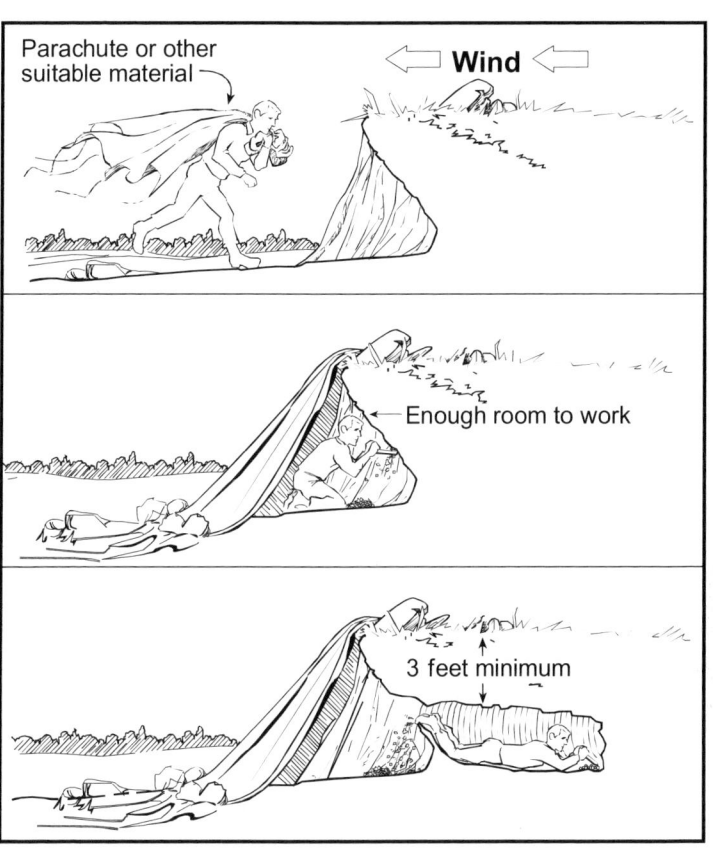

Figure X-2. Improvised Shelter

NUCLEAR EXPLOSIONS: Fall flat. Cover exposed body parts. Present minimal profile to direction of blast. *DO NOT look at fireball!* Remain prone until blast effects are over.

SHELTER: Find, as soon as possible; 5 minutes unsheltered is maximum!

Priority:
(1) Cave or tunnel covered with 3 or more feet of earth.
(2) Storm/storage cellars.
(3) Culverts.
(4) Basements.
(5) Abandoned stone/mud buildings.
(6) Foxhole 4 feet deep (remove topsoil within 2-foot radius of foxhole lip).

RADIATION SHIELDING EFFICIENCIES

Iron/Steel	.7 inches	Cinder Block	5.3 inches	One thickness reduces received radiation dose by half.
Brick	2.0 inches	Ice	6.8 inches	Additional thickness added to any amount of thickness reduces received radiation dose by half.
Concrete	2.2 inches	Wood (Soft)	8.8 inches	
Earth	3.3 inches	Snow	20.3 inches	

SHELTER SURVIVAL: Keep contaminated materials out of shelter.
Good Weather: Bury contaminated clothing outside of shelter (recover later).
Bad Weather: Shake strongly or beat with branches. Rinse and/or shake wet clothing. *DO NOT wring out!*

PERSONAL HYGIENE: Wash entire body with soap and *any* water; give close attention to fingernails and hairy parts.
No Water: Wipe all exposed skin surfaces with clean cloth or uncontaminated soil. Fallout/dusty conditions—keep entire body covered. Keep handkerchief/cloth over mouth and nose. Improvise goggles. *DO NOT smoke!*

DAILY RADIATION TIME TABLE for NO RATE METER

4-6	Complete isolation	9-12	2-4 hours exposure per day
3-7	Brief exposure (30 minutes maximum)	13	Normal movement
8	Brief exposure (1 hour maximum)		

Figure X-3. Radiation Shielding Efficiencies

a. Protection.

1. FIND PROTECTIVE SHELTER IMMEDIATELY!
2. Gather all equipment for survival (time permitting).
3. Avoid detection and capture.
   - Seek existing shelter that may be improved (**Figure X-1**).
   - If no shelter is available, dig a trench or foxhole as follows:
     > Dig trench deep enough for protection, then enlarge for comfort (**Figure X-2**).
     > Cover with available material.
4. Radiation shielding efficiencies (**Figure X-3**).
5. Leave contaminated equipment and clothing near shelter for retrieval after radioactive decay.
6. Lie down, keep warm, sleep, and rest.

b. Substance:

1. Water. Allow no more than thirty minutes exposure on third day for water procurement.
   - Water sources (in order of preference):
     > Springs, wells, or underground sources are safest.
     > Water in pipes/containers in abandoned buildings.
     > Snow (6 or more inches below the surface during the fallout).
     > Streams and rivers (filtered before drinking).
     > Lakes, ponds, pools, etc.
     > Water from below the surface (DO NOT stir up the water).
     > Use a seep well.
   - Water preparation (**Figures X-4** and **X-5**).
     > Filtering through earth removes 99 percent of radioactivity.
     > Purify all water sources.
2. Food.
   - Processed foods (canned or packaged) are preferred; wash and wipe containers before use.

- Animal foods.
  Avoid animals that appear to be sick or dying.
  Skin carefully to avoid contaminating the meat.
  Before cooking, cut meat away from the bone,
      leaving at least 1/8 inch of meat on the bone.
  Discard all internal organs.
  Cook all meat until very well done.
- Avoid.
  Aquatic food sources (use only in extreme
      emergencies because of high concentration
      of radiation).
  Shells of all eggs (contents will be safe to eat).
  Milk from animals.
- Plant foods (in order of preference).
  Plants whose edible portions grow underground
      (for example, potatoes, turnips, carrots, etc.).
      Wash and remove skin.
  Edible portions growing above ground that can
      be washed and peeled or skinned (bananas,
      apples, etc.).
  Smooth-skinned vegetables, fruits, or above-
      ground plants that are not easily peeled or
      washed.

c. Self-aid:
1. General rules:
   - Prevent exposure to contaminants.
   - Use personal hygiene practices and remove body waste from shelter.
   - Rest, avoid fatigue.
   - Drink liquids.
2. Wounds.
   - Clean affected area.
   - Use antibacterial ointment or cleaning solution.
   - Cover with clean dressing.
   - Watch for signs of infection.

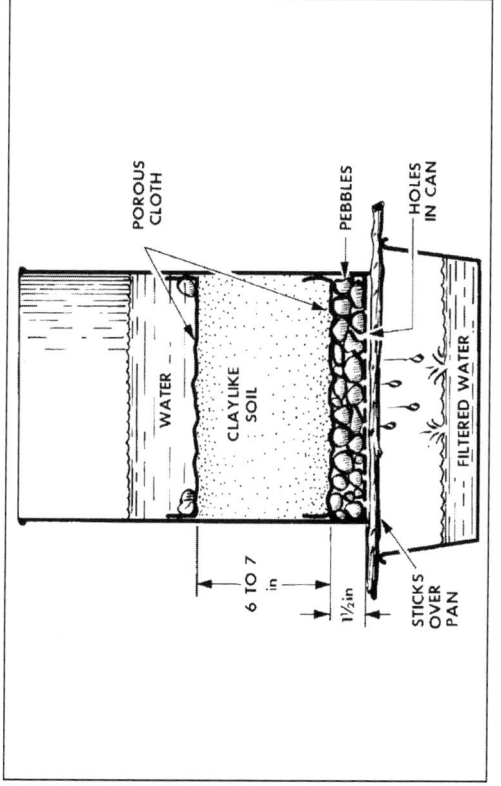

POROUS CLOTH

PEBBLES

HOLES IN CAN

WATER

CLAYLIKE SOIL

FILTERED WATER

6 TO 7 in

1½ in

STICKS OVER PAN

Figure X-4. Filtration Systems, Filtering Water

Figure X-5. Filtration Systems, Settling Water

3. Burns.
   - Clean affected area.
   - Cover with clean dressing.
4. Radiation sickness (nausea, weakness, fatigue, vomiting, diarrhea, loss of hair, radiation burns).
   - Time is required to overcome.
   - Rest.
   - Drink fluids.
   - Maintain food intake.
   - Prevent additional exposure.

2. BIOLOGICAL CONDITIONS

a. Clues that may alert you to a biological attack:
1. Enemy aircraft dropping objects or spraying.
2. Breakable containers or unusual bombs, particularly those bursting with little or no blast, and muffled explosions.
3. Smoke or mist of unknown origin.
4. Unusual substances on the ground or vegetation; sick-looking plants or crops.

b. Protection from biological agents:
1. Use protective equipment.
2. Bathe as soon as the situation permits.
3. Wash hair and body thoroughly with soap and water.
4. Clean thoroughly under fingernails.
5. Clean teeth, gums, tongue, and roof of mouth frequently.

c. Survival tips for biological conditions:
1. Keep your body and living area clean.
2. Stay alert for clues of biological attack.
3. Keep nose, mouth, and skin covered.
4. Keep food and water protected. Bottled or canned

foods are safe if sealed. If in doubt, boil food and water for ten minutes.

5. Construct shelter in a clear area, away from vegetation, with entrance 90 degrees to the prevailing wind.

6. If traveling, travel crosswind or upwind (taking advantage of terrain to stay away from depressions).

3. CHEMICAL CONDITIONS

a. Detecting.

1. Smell. Many agents have little or no odor.
2. Sight. Many agents are colorless:
   - Color. Yellow, orange, or red smoke or mist.
   - Liquid. Oily, dark patches on leaves, ground, etc.
   - Gas. Some agents appear as a mist immediately after shell burst.
   - Solid. Most solid state agents have some color.
3. Sound. Muffled explosions are possible indications of chemical agent bombs.
4. Feel. Irritation to the nose, eyes, or skin and/or moisture on the skin are danger signs.
5. Taste. Strange taste in food or water indicates contamination.
6. General indications. Tears, difficult breathing, choking, itching, coughing, dizziness.
7. Wildlife. Presence of sick or dying animals.

b. Protection against chemical agents:

1. Use protective equipment.
2. Avoid contaminated areas.
   - Exit contaminated area by moving crosswind.
   - Select routes on high ground.
   - Avoid cellars, ditches, trenches, gullies, valleys, etc.

- Avoid woods, tall grasses, and bushes because they tend to hold chemical agent vapors.
- Decontaminate body and equipment as soon as possible by—
     Removing. Pinch-blotting.
     Neutralizing. Warm water.
     Destroying. Burying.

c. Self-aid in chemically contaminated areas.

1. If a chemical defense ensemble is available—
   - Use all protective equipment.
   - Follow antidote directions when needed.
2. If a chemical defense ensemble is not available—
   - Remove or tear away contaminated clothing.
   - Rinse contaminated areas with water.
   - Improvise a breathing filter using materials available (T-shirt, handkerchief, fabric, etc.).

d. Tips for the survivor:

1. DO NOT use wood from a contaminated area for fire.
2. Look for signs of chemical agents around water sources before procurement (oil spots, foreign odors, dead fish, or animals).
3. Keep food and water protected.
4. DO NOT use plants for food or water in contaminated areas.

APPENDIX A

THE WILL TO SURVIVE

ARTICLE VI CODE OF CONDUCT

I will never forget that I am an American fighting for freedom, responsible for my actions, and dedicated to the principles which made my country free. I will trust in my God and in the United States of America.

1. PSYCHOLOGY OF SURVIVAL

a. Preparation.
1. Know your capabilities and limitations.
2. Keep a positive attitude.
3. Develop a realistic plan.
4. Anticipate fears.
5. Combat psychological stress by—
   - Recognizing and anticipating existing stressors (injury, death, fatigue, illness, environment, hunger, isolation).
   - Attributing normal reactions to existing stressors (fear, anxiety, guilt, boredom, depression, anger).
   - Identifying signals of distress created by stressors (indecision, withdrawal, forgetfulness, carelessness, and propensity to make mistakes).

b. Strengthen your will to survive with—
1. The Code of Conduct.
2. Pledge of Allegiance.

3. Faith in America.
4. Patriotic songs.
5. Thoughts of return to family and friends.

c. Group dynamics of survival include—

1. Leadership, good organization, and cohesiveness, which promote high morale:
   - Preventing panic.
   - Creating strength and trust in one another.
   - Favoring persistency in overcoming failure.
   - Facilitating formulation of group goals.
2. Taking care of your buddy.
3. Working as a team.
4. Reassuring and encouraging each other. Influencing factors are—
   - Enforcing the chain of command.
   - Organizing according to individual capabilities.
   - Accepting suggestions and criticism.

2. SPIRITUAL CONSIDERATIONS

a. Collect your thoughts and emotions.
b. Identify your personal beliefs.
c. Use self-control.
d. Meditate.
e. Remember past inner sources to help you overcome adversity.
f. Pray for your God's help, strength, wisdom, and rescue.

1. Talk to your God.
2. Give thanks that God is with you.
3. Ask for God's help.
4. Pray for protection and a positive outcome.

g. Remember scripture, verses, or hymns; repeat them to yourself and to your God.
h. Worship without aid of written scripture, clergy, or others.

i. Forgive—
1. Yourself for what you have done or said that was wrong.
2. Those who have failed you.

j. Praise God and give thanks because—
1. God is bigger than your circumstances.
2. God will see you through (no matter what happens).
3. Hope comes from a belief in heaven and/or an afterlife.

k. Trust.
1. Faith and trust in your God.
2. Love for family and self.
3. Never lose hope.
4. Never give up.

l. With other survivors—
1. Identify or appoint a religious lay leader.
2. Discuss what is important to you.
3. Share scriptures and songs.
4. Pray for each other.
5. Try to have worship services.
6. Write down scriptures and songs that you remember.
7. Encourage each other while waiting for rescue; remember—
   • Your God loves you.
   • Praise your God.

INDEX

twist sticks, 86, 87

ABOUT THE AUTHOR

Sergeant First Class Matt Larsen, a longtime trainer in survival and fighting techniques for the Army Rangers, previously updated the *U.S. Army Survival Handbook* (Lyons Press). He is Director of the Modern Army Combatives Program and commandant of the U. S. Army Combatives School. A graduate of the multiservice SERE (Survival, Evasion, Rescue, and Escape) training program, he served in the 75th Ranger Regiment for over twelve years, parachuting into Panama during the invasion there and participating in the Gulf War. Larsen resides in Columbus, Georgia.